SHE IS AN OVERCOMER

Real Women, Real Stories – Inspiring You to Overcome Your Challenges

SHE IS AN OVERCOMER

Real Women, Real Stories – Inspiring You to Overcome Your Challenges

Dara Bose & Lynda Sunshine West

Action Takers Publishing™
San Diego, California

Action Takers Publishing™
www.actiontakerspublishing.com

Paperback ISBN: 978-1-956665-15-4
ebook ISBN: 978-1-956665-12-3

Library of Congress Control Number: 2022914994

Cover Design by Sam Art Studio
Printed in the United States of America

TABLE OF CONTENTS

This book is dedicated to the woman who feels broken and alone; we see you and we understand that feeling. You are not alone.

A SUNNY NOTE FROM DARA BOSE AND LYNDA SUNSHINE WEST

"For whatever is born of God overcomes the world; and this is the victory that has overcome the world—our faith. Who is the one who overcomes the world, but he who believes that Jesus is the Son of God?"
~1 John 5:4-5

This book was truly a calling from God. Dara was working with Lynda Sunshine on another book when the idea for this book came to her. She pitched the idea, and *She Is an Overcomer* was born.

Every person has their own unique life experiences as well as their own struggles and triumphs. The 31 women in this book prove that. They share their stories in their own words and from a place of vulnerability. These are the real stories of real women who have lived through challenges that many people may or may not have faced at some point in their lives. For some of these women, writing was a form of therapy, while, for others, it was difficult as it caused them to relive traumatic experiences.

When we brought together this amazing group of women, we wanted to be sure that we did not limit the types of stories that were being told. There could be a woman out there thinking that she is alone and that no one could understand how she felt. She could feel like there is no hope for her. These women are here to tell you that there is hope.

TRIGGER WARNING

Triggers are anything that might cause a person to recall a traumatic experience they've had. For example, graphic images of violence might be a trigger for some people, but not others. Less obvious things, including songs, odors, or even colors, can also be triggers, depending on someone's experiences. Some of the stories in this book might cause you to remember a traumatic experience or event from your past and may lead to heightened emotions. This can be called a "trigger." If this happens to you, there is help out there and you can find it if you need it. The women in this book are simply telling their stories after much healing has taken place in their own lives.

Chapter 1

LIFE AFTER SUICIDE

by Dara Bose

I was about 16 years old the first time I had a 'breakdown,' but it would not be the last time.

It was just a typical evening. My family had just finished dinner and I retreated into my room like a typical 16-year-old. As I was standing in my bedroom, my heart began to race. The thumping of my own heartbeat sounded like a swarm of angry bees buzzing around in my head. It was almost deafening and caused a pressure in my ears that made it feel like my head was going to explode. It felt like an elephant was sitting on my chest and with each breath the air grew thinner and thinner. My lungs were on fire. My body felt hot and cold all at the same time. I was numb all over, yet could feel every nerve in my body screaming. My body was shaking uncontrollably and hot tears streamed down my face. I could taste the saltiness of the tears and feel their heat, but I did not even know I was crying. A flood of emotions came crashing over me like violent waves of the ocean. Each wave was a new emotion, some of which I had never felt before. I could not see what was coming next. I was lost in a hurricane of spiraling, uncontrollable emotions. They were now in control. It felt as though I had come out of my own body and was witnessing this emotional hurricane from outside of myself. I had ZERO control.

All I could think as I was watching this happen to me was, 'this is it! I am going to die.'

It seemed as if I was never going to regain control of my body but, eventually, I did. My mom and my stepdad had no idea what to make of my episode. I was sure I had lost my mind and gone crazy. A trip to the doctor a couple of days later revealed that I had an anxiety attack. My official diagnosis was anxiety and depression. I was given a prescription for anti-depressants and sent on my way. Throughout the years, I have been on and off depression and anxiety medications. There are times when things get to be too much for me to handle and I require a little more help, and that's okay. It's okay to need help when struggling. It is NOT okay to stay quiet about it and suffer on your own. If you are struggling, ask for help, whether it be prayer, friends or family, a pastor, therapy, or a doctor. The **24/7 Crisis Hotline at 1-800-273-TALK (8255)** is always ready to help.

Growing up, my parents struggled. My mom was only 17 when she got pregnant with me and dropped out of High School. My dad was 25 and worked for the United States Postal Service. We lived in a mobile home in a rural community outside of the city. Even at a young age, I could tell that my parents were stressed. My sister was born when I was three and a half. Having two small children, a home, and all the financial strains that come with it took a toll on my parents. My father's drug addiction did not help matters much either. When I was around age five, my parents divorced. I was furious with my mother for taking us from our home and my dad from me. As a five-year-old, I could not understand that what she was doing was what was best for her, and for my sister and me. My dad has his own demons and my mom was trying to protect us from them. In fact, my first real memory that I have of my childhood is not a pleasant one.

The thing about demons is that sometimes they can affect the ones we love. One night that demon knocked on our door. My sister was still a baby and had already been put to bed in my parents' room. I can remember her bassinet sitting in the living room, where I was sitting with my mom and dad watching TV before bed. I wasn't more than four years old at the time and I can still see the terror in my parents' eyes when the pounding on the door started. My dad answered and an oversized man was standing in the doorway. His voice was low and mean. I could tell that this man was not my dad's friend by the tone and the words they were using. My mom told me to go to my room and began to rush me towards the hallway. The large man began to yell at my dad. Just as my mom pushed me into the bedroom, my sister's bassinet flew across the living room and crashed at the opening of the hallway, just a few feet from my bedroom door. I cannot recall all of what the man said, but the thing I do remember is the man telling my dad, "if you don't pay what you owe, I'm going to come back and kill your wife and kids and make you watch, before I kill you…"

After the divorce, my sister and I lived with our mom and stepdad, visiting our dad every other weekend. On the weekends we spent with our dad, our mom would drop us off at our grandma's house on Friday night and our dad would pick us up on Saturday after he got off of work. Our grandmother was Catholic and would often take us to mass on the weekends we were there. On the weekends we were at home with our mom, I would go to a Baptist church and youth group with my childhood best friend and her family. Visiting different denominations of Christianity during my youth was confusing at times. The one thing that remained constant was I knew I wanted to know more about God and be closer to Him. I felt loved, cared for, and, most of all, safe in the presence of the Lord. One day during worship the Pastor was talking about being saved and how much the Lord loved us. He then called anyone forward that wanted to accept God into his or her life. I was overwhelmed with this feeling that I cannot describe. It was almost as if the Lord had reached out and touched my heart. I walked up to the front of the church crying and could not speak. I had been called. I was ready to be baptized. It was the beginning of the summer between 8th grade and freshman year. My youth pastor from the local Baptist church I had been attending came and met with my mom and stepdad. We made all the plans and arrangements for my baptism the following weekend. A few days later, I was struck down with illness. I had mono. I was sick for the entire summer break. By the time I had finally recovered it was time to start the school year and, before I knew it, I began drifting away from my faith and that feeling began to fade. Other things began to take up my time and priority.

Years passed by and my life moved on. Marriage, kids, and jobs kept me busy, but something always felt like it was missing. I was struggling with my depression. Like my dad, I had my own demons. My demons were different, yet the struggles were similar.

On the morning of January 25, 2013, I was making phone calls and answering text messages about a gathering I was having at my house that evening. One of my friends was there helping me prepare for the party. In the middle of all of the hustle, I received a call from my stepsister telling me about an accident on the train tracks and my dad being involved. I was having trouble understanding what she was trying to tell me. Partly, because she never calls me and partly because my brain could not comprehend the words she was stringing together. So I asked her again, "What do you mean dad had an accident on the train tracks? Did his truck stall out or something? Is he okay?" I was rattling off questions faster than the words could spring from my mouth. That is when she stopped me. She explained again, "Dara, dad didn't make it." This time I understood. Dad had an accident on the tracks and he was gone. Although I now understood her words, I still could not grasp the entire story.

After I hung up the phone my mind started to retrace the words she was telling me. I started to piece together memories of the last couple of days in my head. I remembered the conversation I had with my dad just two days before. He called me on Wednesday to talk, which was not unusual. We did not talk every day, but when a couple weeks would pass one of us would at least reach out to the other to see how things were going. Over the past few months, he had been the one to reach out because I was busy with my new baby. So, when he had called me, I did not think much of it. It was a pretty normal call. He asked me how I was feeling, about the kids, and my husband. We chatted for a while about everything going on with my family. He told me that he was really depressed and I told him that I understood how he felt. At the time, he had recently retired from his job and was facing another divorce. He had been married to my stepmom since I was very young. I knew he was struggling with it and did not want to get divorced. I also knew that his demons from my childhood still plagued him. I did find it odd that he had asked me several times about my husband's work schedule. You see, my husband, Bob, is a firefighter/paramedic and his call area covers my dad's small town. My dad kept asking when Bob worked and what time he got off. He knew that Bob worked 24-hour shifts, yet he asked about it several times. I explained to him that Bob worked tomorrow (Thursday) at 7:00am and got off at 7:00am on Friday. I found it weird that he was dwelling on this. He again asked, "So, Bob gets off at seven on Friday morning?" Although I found it odd at the time, I again reassured him. We ended the call with "I love you's" and him sending his love to Bob and each of our kids.

I did not know it at the time, but he had a plan. He lived next to those train tracks for most of my life and he knew the train schedule. He was making sure that my husband would not be on shift on Friday when the train came through. He was finalizing his plans. He was saying goodbye. That was the last time I would ever hear his voice. He was so lost in his own darkness that he could not see a way out. My dad took his own life on January 25, 2013.

The world came crashing in around me. I once again found myself lost in a swirling hurricane of emotions. I could not breathe. I was spiraling into an anxiety attack, but I had to pull myself together. I had to call my husband, my sister, and my mom. My husband could not even understand me on the phone, but as he rushed home from his second job he saw the emergency vehicles from his department and began to piece it all together. Over the next few hours, I felt I had told so many people that I became numb. My husband was taking care of the kids and my friend that was there helped me make all the cancelations for the party that was supposed to be that night.

I retreated to my room to find some peace. In those moments, I started to go through the *what-ifs. What if I would have called him more? What if I would have called him last night and invited him to the comedy show? (I had an extra ticket.) What if... what if...* After the *what-ifs* came the anger. *How can he do this to us? Were we not enough for him to want to stay? Did he not really love us? Did he even care how this would make us feel?* Then came the blame. *How did I not know that he was this deep? How did I not see that he was thinking about suicide? He told me he was depressed! I should have seen it.* As a survivor of suicide, the ones left behind typically face cycles of *what-ifs*, anger, blame, grief, and more all the time. Sometimes it will even come out of nowhere.

Hundreds of people showed up for his funeral. The line was so long that they ended up having to just close the doors. He fought his demons for my entire life. Many people probably never saw it. He was always so full of life. I think he wanted to make sure others did not feel the pain that he felt, so he spent his time entertaining others and making them smile. After the funeral, I knew that I needed to seek help for myself. I knew that my depression was heavier than I could handle on my own, so I talked with my doctor and got back on anti-depressants.

The medication helped me for a while. It definitely took the edge off, but some days were still hard. Losing someone to suicide leaves a mark on you. I have lost family and friends to vehicle accidents and cancer, but there is just something about suicide that hits differently. So many unanswered questions.

In the years following the loss of my dad, I decided to go back to school and finish my degree in accounting. I ended up getting a great job before I finished my degree and stopped going to school. I mean, I already had the job, so what was the point. From there I ended up landing my 'dream job.' You know the one that society tells you that you need in order to be successful. I had the fancy title, the nice office, and the big paycheck. Yet, I still felt like something was missing. It wasn't just to loss of my dad. It was something deeper.

I tried all the things to try to fill the void. To be honest, I was heading down a dark path. I was drinking more than I care to admit. I was always angry and irritated. One day I was self-medicating with a bottle of wine while scrolling social media when it finally hit me. I realized that if I continued on this path I was on I would ruin my marriage and my kids would hate me. I had to make a change and that night God put me back on the right path. He showed me that happiness comes from within and that it was up to me to make the choice to be happy. Fulfillment comes from a life with Jesus, but He also knew that my redirection needed a different approach. It started with my joining a direct sales company and diving into personal development.

Over the next few months, I learned a lot about myself and started to understand my purpose. I knew that my 'dream job' was bringing me down and holding me back, but what was I to do? I needed to have the income to help support my family. But, God had a plan. That direct sales business I had joined was making extra income, but it was not enough to supplement it fully. I prayed for the answer. I prayed that God would show me the path. I knew if I stayed where I was, things could not improve.

My husband and I have three kids and with both of us being working parents, my mother-in-law took care of the kids before and after school. Over the past few years, her health had been deteriorating. In June of 2018, my mother-in-law had a stroke. It was pretty severe and she had to go to a nursing home. Since she was the caregiver for our kids while we worked, I had to make a change. My God does not make bad things happen, but He can certainly make something good come from them.

I talked to my employer about the possibility of working from home to finish the summer and then changing my schedule to accommodate school days when my husband was on shift. My boss almost laughed in my face at the idea. So, I started looking for new employment. Most of the jobs I looked at would not have worked out for one reason or another, too little pay, too much travel. Then my best friend happened to look at her church's website and there was a posting for a part-time church accountant; it was PERFECT!

I applied for the position and was offered the job. The hours were Monday-Thursday 9:00am-3:00pm. I could get my kids on the bus in the morning and make it home in time to get them off of the bus. God had answered my prayer. He got me out of a job that was making me a person that I did not want to be. He put me into a job where I could be myself and grow in my faith, but most of all... He was setting me up for my true purpose.

My title and position at the church started off as the part-time church accountant, but has grown into a full-time position with many titles and responsibilities. The more I got involved in the church and the more I grew in my faith, the more ME I became. And then more JOY and GRATITUDE filled my life. My void was filled. BUT, I still felt called for more. I kept feeling like God was calling me to do more. I was working full time, leading small groups, coaching in my business, as well as writing. What more could I do?

One day, while my husband and I were on vacation in the mountains of Tennessee, we were sitting around a fire chatting. He was asking me questions about my book and how he could help me in my business. Then it happened. It just came flying out of my mouth. I said, "I feel like God is calling me to be a pastor. I think I have been holding back because I am afraid of what that means." There it was! It was out there now. He was 100% supportive. So, on the way back home from our trip, I reached out to one of my pastors to find out the next steps. It was real now.

So as I write this, I am now re-enrolled in college and pursuing a degree in Psychology. When I am finished, I will go on to Seminary. I am still discerning if that is a call to pastor a church or focus on pastoral counseling, but I know I am letting go and letting God lead me. We do not have to know all the answers to move forward on the path that God has laid before us. We just have to be brave enough and faithful enough to put one foot in front of the other. Even when we feel like Moses, wandering in the wilderness, we must remember Jeremiah 29:11.

"For I know the plans I have for you," Declares the Lord. "Plans to prosper you and not harm you, plans to give you hope and a future."
Jeremiah 29:11

In the darkness of my mental health struggle and the loss of my dad, there were days where I could not see the light. I felt consumed by the emptiness, overcome by my own demons, and drowned in the blame. Honestly, if I had not lost my dad the way I did, it could have been me. I fought some of the same demons. I too felt the darkness call to me. Losing my dad was one of the darkest days of my life, but realizing that I had the strength to pull myself out of the darkness that he could not, gave me hope. I heard God calling to me but holding onto all of the pain was just easier at times. I needed Him and I needed forgiveness. Once I accepted that God back into my life, I was able to forgive my dad for leaving us and I was able to forgive myself for being angry with him and stop blaming myself. I was able to forgive myself for choices that I had made. There are still hard days, but I have a certain comfort in my faith.

I never thought I would be where I am today. I was the girl from the wrong side of the tracks, whose family was on food stamps, her dad was a drug addict, she drank more than she should, she had depression, and her dad committed suicide. It could have been me. I could have continued down a path of destruction and who knows where I could have ended up. My dad lost his way in the darkness, but I found the light. I survived and I will live on when he could not. Out of his darkness, I found the light.

DARA BOSE

Dara Bose is a certified NLP Practitioner, Life Coach, international bestselling author, and public speaker. She has spent years working on personal development while reaching top rankings in the MLM industry. Through her work in MLM, she discovered her passion for building up other women and her purpose to help them thrive. The wife of a firefighter and mother of three, Dara never ceases to amaze with finding time to support and uplift women in her community.

Whether through participating in small groups at church, organizing fundraising events, and everything in between, Dara represents her best self in all she does. She motivates women to seek their best self through self-reflection, motivation, fashion, and friendship. Women seek her out for guidance regularly when working through difficult times, or just needing the support of another woman/mother/wife/business owner. Constantly seeking to better herself and provide the best support she can for others, you can always find her reading a book or attending seminars that build her up and better equip her to share her messaging.

Dara is best known for her saying she uses regularly with her children and friends, and can also be applied to anyone in most all situations - "But did you die?" Most importantly, Dara wants all women to know, you are worthy, you are beautiful, and you are meant for more.

Connect with Dara at https://darabose.com/.

Chapter 2

FAITH OVER FEAR WINS EVERY TIME

by Lynda Sunshine West

Faith
Erases
Anxious
Reactions
~Lynda Sunshine West

When your fear is strong, your faith is weak; when your faith is strong, your fear is weak.

In 2015, I did something a little crazy. I embarked on a journey like no other, a journey that would test my faith in myself, my faith in those in my sphere of influence and, most importantly, my faith in God, on a daily basis. That journey led to me uncovering things that I didn't know about myself and it would put me on a path of growth, courage, strength, perseverance, desire, passion, drive, and so many more positive and uplifting words.

What did I do?

Well, something was different that early morning of January 1, 2015. I woke up that morning (just like every day before that) and had an epiphany, an illuminating discovery, a shift in my mindset, a thought that would forever change the trajectory of my life. I had no idea what was to come, but I knew something was going to be different.

It was like that lightbulb that goes off in your brain, the lightbulb that you know without a doubt that you HAVE to turn on or you will lose that idea forever. It will be cast to the wind and travel through the atmosphere for someone else to do something with. You know what I'm talking about. That "I HAVE to do this RIGHT NOW" feeling because the magnetic pull is so strong that you know if you don't do it right now you'll live to regret it. Yep, that's how it felt for me.

That epiphany went something like this.

"I have so many fears and my fears are stopping me from living my life. I know that I have to do something different this year, something that will stretch me to become the person God meant me to be, not the person I am today. I've gotta change my life. Here's what I'm going to do. I'm going to face a fear every day for an entire year. Every morning when I wake up, the first thing I'm going to do before my feet hit the bed is ask myself one question, 'What scares me?' and then I'll wait for the answer. I won't get out of bed until an answer comes. The first fear that pops into my head is the fear I am COMMITTED to facing that day."

They say, "The definition of insanity is doing the same thing over and over again and expecting different results." That was me. That was how I lived the previous 51 years of my life, expecting different results from not doing anything, not stepping outside of my comfort zone. Well, that's just not how the universe works.

When I made that declaration to myself, to commit to breaking through one fear every day for a year, I had no idea what the next 365 days would hold for me and how tapped into my faith it would bring me.

"Why would someone decide to face a fear every day for a year?" "Did you really have that many fears?" "What kind of fears did you face?" "What was it like?" These are a few of the questions I hear when I talk about The Year of Fears. I'll answer a few of them here and, as I share my story, you'll see how faith played a HUGE part in breaking through fear every day and how it changed my life.

I grew up in an extremely volatile, abusive alcoholic household. The abuse caused a lot of pain, heartache, fear, I became a people-pleaser and, worst of all, I not only acquired a tremendous fear of judgment, but I became extremely judgmental. Motivational Speaker Jim Rohn famously said, "We are the average of the five people we spend the most time." (If you're judgmental, you're most likely hanging out with judgmental people and it's time to find some new friends.) While I carried all of that pain around with me for decades, being a people-pleaser was my worst attribute. I used to pride myself in being "a chameleon." I could blend into any situation and everyone liked me. That was my survival mechanism. Be quiet. Blend in. Don't make a raucous. Sit in the corner. Don't bother anyone. Don't make a scene. As a people-pleaser, I never knew who Lynda was. Since I wanted everyone to like me, I did and said what I "thought" you wanted me to do so you would like me.

This was one of the things I discovered while facing a fear every day that year. When you gain awareness of yourself, that's when change can occur. Until then, you'll live your life hiding behind who you could be rather than stepping into the light and being who you are meant to be, serving your purpose while on this ball called earth.

Part of my fear-facing was learning who I am, speaking up for myself, saying yes when I wanted to say yes, and learning how to say no. Boy!! That was the scariest thing, saying no to people. While I knew it was going to be hard, I did it BECAUSE I was scared. "Do it BECAUSE you're scared, Lynda Sunshine," became my new mantra.

My faith was tested on a daily basis. Faith of self. Faith of others. Faith of God.

Faith of God and faith of others was easy, but faith of self? I had to learn how to believe in myself so I could have faith that I could conquer the challenges before me, the 365 fears I was about to embark upon.

Growing up in an abusive environment where the people I'm supposed to be able to trust said terrible things to me on a daily basis like "you're stupid," "you're ignorant," "people are only nice to you because they feel sorry for you," really did a number on my mindset. The worst part was that not only did people in my life say those mean things to me, but I became my own worst enemy and beat myself up mentally better than anyone else ever could. When I sensed that one of those pesky boys in junior high school was going to call me a name or make fun of me, I didn't give him the satisfaction. I made fun of myself first and beat him to it. What I didn't know at that time, though, was that by beating myself up mentally for so many years, I was creating within me a lack of self-confidence and a belief that I had no value.

So, when 2015 came around and I made a declaration to break through one fear every day for a year, I was bound and determined to change that mindset once and for all no matter how hard it was.

One day when I woke up and asked myself that daily question, "What scares me?," the fear that popped into my head was very specific: "approach and talk to a stranger in Starbucks®."

You see, like many entrepreneurs, I had been using my local Starbucks® as a remote office for a few years. And I'm not even a coffee drinker. Every time I showed up at Starbucks®, I would find a place to set up my "office." I'd immediately pull out my laptop, start working, and intentionally not make eye contact with anyone. While it may seem like a small, even silly, fear, it was a crippling fear for me. Fear is fear no matter how you slice it. My decision to face a fear every day for a year was a commitment to myself for growth. And boy did I grow!

So, that day, when I was challenged to talk to a stranger in Starbucks®, I walked into the store, stood in a corner and watched people come in, place their order, and leave with their coffee. After about 10 agonizing minutes of waiting for a stranger to come in, one man came in, placed his order, and then he sat down. Yes, my victim!

My target was a person sitting alone so I could have a conversation with them. And there he was: alone, sitting, waiting for his coffee. I was finally going to face this fear. I stood there, staring at him, desperately trying to come up with my "opening line" of the conversation. "Heck, Lynda, it's not a date. It's just a conversation," I said to myself as I was getting all worked up about talking to a stranger.

After he picked up his coffee and returned to his table, I slowly walked over to him, knees trembling, throat locked up, palms and forehead sweaty, stomach all knotted up. Praying my voice would not fail me, I managed to say, "Hi, sir. I'm facing a fear every day this year. And today's fear is to talk to a stranger in Starbucks®." He responded suspiciously good-humored, "Okay!?"

So far, so good. I got the words out of my mouth in a coherent manner and he responded.

"Do you mind if I have a seat?"

"Sure. Please have a seat."

I chatted with him for about five minutes, stood up and said, "Thank you for your time. You helped me break through this fear. I appreciate it." I turned and walked out of Starbucks®. I felt like throwing up. But I didn't.

I did it. I tapped into my faith of self. I broke through that fear, the fear of judgment.

God was always there to help me, but I needed to do the work. I just hadn't been ready until 2015, age 51. It's all good, though, because it's part of my journey, my story. I know now that all of the things I went through are what created who I am today. I, for the first time in my life, love myself FOR WHO I AM. I have always had faith in God, but I finally have faith in me.

While faith in God will carry us far, faith in ourselves will carry us further because we're willing to take more risks and put ourselves out there more.

They say, "Turn your pain into your purpose." One of the greatest blessings I received from facing 365 fears is discovering my purpose and then living "on purpose" rather than "on accident" (like I had the first 51 years of my life).

Once I started believing in myself and raising my hand to share my voice with the world, I was met with praise. That's when I discovered I am not stupid and ignorant like they told me I was. Rather I am brilliant and people actually like me because I'm a nice person, not because they feel sorry for me. This was a huge part of my journey because when I started raising my hand and speaking my truth, others started doing the same. They saw what I was doing and it gave them FAITH that they, too, could do it. They started walking their path and speaking up for themselves.

When we share our story with the world, it gives others confidence and courage to do the same thing, the confidence and courage to stand up for themselves and to tap into their faith of God, faith of others, and, most importantly, faith of self. When we have faith in ourselves, there's nothing stopping us. Sometimes it takes an outsider to guide us onto that path. Who is that person for you? Reach out to them right now. Don't wait another day. They will help you tap into your faith so you can start living your life "on purpose."

Faith is felt, not seen. It's such an interesting concept to me because, while it's not tangible to the touch, it is tangible in the heart. If we don't understand something, it's hard to believe in it; therefore, we believe based on facts or faith. Sometimes faith is all we have to guide us.

I ask you, "How strong is your faith in self, in others, in God?"

Be brave and share your weaknesses, for in your weaknesses,
others see your strengths.
~Lynda Sunshine West

LYNDA SUNSHINE WEST

She ran away at 5 years old and was gone an entire week. She came home riddled with fears and became a people-pleaser. At age 51, she decided to face one fear every day for an entire year. In doing so, she gained an exorbitant amount of confidence and now uses what she learned to fulfill her mission to empower 5 million women and men to share their stories with the world to make a greater impact on the planet.

Lynda Sunshine West is the Founder and CEO of Action Takers Publishing, a Speaker, 16 Times #1 International Bestselling and Award-Winning Author, Executive Film Producer, and Red Carpet Interviewer.

She believes in cooperation and collaboration and loves connecting with like-minded people.

She proudly donates a percentage of her profits to The Giving Angels, a 501(c)(3) nonprofit.

Ready to share your story and join an anthology book like this?

Connect with Lynda Sunshine at www.actiontakerspublishing.com

Chapter 3

RISING FROM THE ASHES

by Aliscia Brorman

Growing up in the foster system introduced me to trauma, betrayal, anxiety, depression, abuse in all forms, abandonment and, last but not least, I learned from an early age that there is, in fact, evil in this world. Believe it or not, growing up in the foster system also introduced me to coping mechanisms, survival skills, independence, problem-solving techniques, and even the art of persuasion. Every hardship, every life-changing event, and every single experience that I endured was meant to turn my mess into my message. In 2 Timothy 4:7 Paul declares, "I have fought the good fight, I have finished the race, I have kept the faith." I developed a deep connection to this verse as I felt abandoned, betrayed, and left to figure out this cruel world on my own. I felt like a caterpillar who was constantly getting caught up in a web of lies and deceit, but with Christ on my side, I was able to blossom into the butterfly who now soars much higher and further than I ever could have imagined.

In 2005, I was placed into the foster system for the second time in my life. I was an energetic 7-year-old girl who quickly learned how to turn on my happy face at school even though home life was a daily struggle. When I was placed back into the foster system, it became much more difficult to act as if I had a life with no problems. This difficulty was not due to my inability to put on my happy face but rather it was the fact that we were only allowed to have three shirts and two pairs of pants in our possession at the group home. No matter how big of a smile I put on my face, there was no way to distract young girls from the fact that I was constantly wearing the same shirt and pants in one week and every week after. So on top of the trauma experienced at home, being ripped away from my family, and being placed in an unknown shelter with unfamiliar faces, I had to add bullying to the list of adversity I was currently experiencing.

The problem-solving techniques I was forced to develop from an early age kicked right into gear. I had the girls throw their clothes into a pile and I went to work mix-matching them all so that we could get on a rotation that made it appear as if we had more clothes than we did. My solution to the problem fueled my passion for fashion. I soon grew out of the clothes I brought with me to the group home and was given the opportunity to go buy new clothes. Funding for group homes was scarce, so our clothes were always new to us, but never truly new. We were taken to the local thrift stores to obtain our next set of clothes. This introduction was the start of a journey to last a lifetime.

As I strolled through the aisles of the thrift stores, I couldn't help but feel a deep connection to the clothes as they, too, had once been loved and cared for, but now hang there forgotten, all the while waiting for someone to decide they were worthy of a home. My love for thrifting never faded.

One day, the Hebrews 12:1 verse caught my attention, "run with endurance the race that is set before us." As I read this, I couldn't help but think that I was being called to advocate for the children who were going through similar experiences as I. It was 2016 when I felt that it was my time to shed light on a topic that is oftentimes left in the dark. I decided to combine my love for thrifting with my passion for advocacy. This combination was the foundation for my idea to open a store that showcases chic vintage finds. The Forgotten Youth a.k.a TFY Apparel made its first debut in my idea book.

Five years passed in the blink of an eye. Not a day went by that I didn't think about TFY, but I was crippled by my desire for perfection. I refused to bring the idea to life simply because I was waiting for the perfect day. I always came up with some new excuse as to why I wasn't ready or why the time just wasn't quite right. Nonetheless, I continued thrifting and acquiring beautiful pieces everywhere that I traveled. My collection grew so large that I ended up turning the master bedroom in my two-bedroom house into my closet. Despite my growing inventory, I still never felt as though it was the "right time." While I was worried about logistics and target audiences all those years, I was standing by as little to no change was being made within the foster system.

On November 14, 2021, my entire outlook and mindset was shaken at its core. That is the day I gave birth to my beautiful baby boy. While I was pregnant, I was so concerned with the life I would be bringing this child into. Am I stable enough? Will I be able to show unconditional love even though I lacked a good example of the meaning of it? How do I ensure his life never endures hardship like my own? So many things raced through my mind as I prepared to bring a precious life into this world. After being abandoned and abused, I wanted to ensure I was bringing him into a world where I could protect him from all of the cruelty in the world. I never felt that I was truly prepared to be a mother. However, ready or not, the day approached rapidly. From the moment that I looked into the eyes of my child I knew that I would break the cycle of abuse and provide a foundation of stability and faith that will ensure that he is happy, healthy, and most importantly, never forgotten. At that moment, my outlook shifted on what it meant to be prepared for something. I realized that while preparation is key, I had to be the person to insert the key into the hole to unlock the door to success. I understood that in order to give my son the life I so longed to give him, I had to take action and allow God to guide me as I made choices in my everyday life. In the same way, I could no longer sit around overthinking minor details for TFY because It was time to take action and trust that God would guide me to the doors that he intended for me to open.

I remember the day that I hit the ground running. It was February 28th, 2022. This was the day that I sold my very first home. It was the day that I recognized that I had, despite my best efforts of denial, been experiencing postpartum depression. It was also the day that I broke free from that postpartum depression. The amount of motivation and passion that I felt towards TFY had never been stronger. I began getting photographs taken of the clothing, creating my website, and establishing a business entity all within the same week. I knew God was calling on me to spread awareness and advocate for change for his children that were being forgotten.

I am currently residing in the state of Texas where the foster system has been in a crisis for over a decade. The state has been housing foster children inside Child Protective Services offices on nothing more than a cot. The workers are overloaded with cases, and oftentimes become so overwhelmed that they simply cannot take it any longer. The lack of funding is the core issue. Texas has been unable to become compliant with the Family First Prevention Services Act of 2018 which has disqualified the state from receiving the funding that comes along with the implementation of the Act. Texas is in the middle of a lawsuit that claims that Texas is violating the constitutional rights of foster children by depriving them of adequate living conditions and health care. According to court documents, the Texas Department of Family and Protective Services stands to lose a total amounting to $43 million in federal funding between 2022-2023 all because we are unable to become compliant.

If there was ever a time for me to try to remove the veil of ignorance from the faces of people who simply are unaware or blind to this historic, decade-long crisis, it is now. There is an obvious need for change in the system, and the status quo has remained stagnant for far too long. With every shirt I sell and every story I am able to tell, I pray that I am planting a seed of awareness that will blossom into change. TFY Apparel is meant to be a steppingstone that helps cultivate relationships, spread awareness about a broken system, and also produce revenue so that I can open up a nonprofit organization that seeks to assist transitioning foster youth and advocate for political and social change in the system. Although I wanted to jump straight into the nonprofit, I recognized that there were steppingstones I had to cross prior. TFY is the first steppingstone for me. If it weren't for the many trials that I faced as a young girl, this motivation I have now to advocate for the forgotten youth of our society may have never existed. When I am asked how I remain one of God's warriors my response is always, "How could I not? He was protecting me throughout the trauma I was experiencing all the while preparing me for the battle ahead."

At the end of the day, no matter how much independence I gained from being in the foster system, I recognize that I cannot do this alone. I was listening to a podcast show called "Foster Strong" when one of their members laid out an analogy that stuck with me. I once was being fed by the system. I now intend to help feed the children of tomorrow by promoting change for them through my voice. Will you help? There are so many ways to make a change. Whether donating clothes to a local children's shelter, volunteering one day at a group home, or setting up an event for the youth, the possibilities are endless. For too long foster youth have been left in the dark. It is time to let God's light shine through so that together we can all work towards change.

I fully intend to run this race that God has set before me until I return home to Him. I believe that God has a way of turning our worst nightmares into our best daydreams. Without experiencing the abandonment, I would not have found a deep connection to thrifting.

Without the limitations of the group home on clothing, I would not have developed my passion for fashion. Without abuse and neglect, I would not have a story that resonates with the foster youth that I mentor. Without my mess, I would have no message. I feel that it is my job to be the voice for the voiceless and allow God to guide my voice so that I am able to stand as firm as Paul did in his last days to know that I, too, fought the good fight, finished the race, and kept the faith.

ALISCIA BRORMAN

Aliscia Brorman is a former foster youth who has exceeded the world's expectations. She is a part of the less than 3% of foster youth who not only graduate high school, but also go on to graduate from college. Aliscia wears several different hats ranging from being a real estate agent by day and mom to a spunky 8-month-old by night. She is also a small business owner of a chic vintage resell store where she utilizes the platform she created to spread awareness and advocate for change within the broken foster system. Aliscia uses her voice to promote change in many ways. She uses her public speaking as a way to incentivize communities to initiate change locally, while also mentoring foster youth who will soon be aging out of the system. Aliscia hopes to be able to empower, uplift, and validate the forgotten youth within our country while also calling to action the policymakers and leaders of every community to step up and be a part of the revitalization of a broken system. One of her core beliefs is that everyone has the ability to create their own reality. Aliscia is living proof that while your past has already been written, it is up to you to write what comes next.

Connect with Aliscia at www.tfyapparel.com.

Chapter 4

OVERCOMING OBSTACLES

by Ashley Paul

We will all face obstacles at some point in our lives. How do you handle it when it doesn't go as planned? Where do you turn when the people around you don't understand your different experience? Or when you realize the obstacle in front of you is bigger to carry than you could ever have imagined?

There is not a day that goes by that I am not thankful for the opportunity to become a mom. Raising two beautiful girls that shine brighter than the sun itself is a blessing. Their energy, creativity and love for the world are amazing little slices of heaven in our everyday lives. Yes, being a parent can be exhausting, challenging, and overwhelming, but my husband and I can both attest that it is the best and hardest thing we've ever done. As challenging as it can be, it is also full of deep laughter, heart filling joy, and an immense amount of gratitude. We wouldn't trade it for the world, even the hard moments.

We see all the beauty in bringing a child into this world. Our culture has set the standard as something we congratulate and celebrate in every part of the experience. It is wonderful and we should celebrate that little life that we have been blessed with.

However, there is a portion of this life experience that does not get much light shed on it. At least not enough light. We do not often hear about the challenges that are overcome on a daily basis by moms in their birth experience or the months following. We don't talk enough about the struggles with body image, healing, depression, anxiety, or judgment that we battle. We don't shine enough light on the hard moments.

When there is a lack of conversation around the challenges in conjunction with the blessings, we miss opportunities to come alongside other moms and encourage them. We have the ability to make other moms feel seen and heard in all the amazing AND difficult moments. We have an opportunity to help them not feel alone when their experience doesn't fit this vision that is created.

With our first daughter, my pregnancy was fairly easy, and the C-section went really well. My husband and I climbed a lighthouse the day before I went in for my C-section – that's how good I was feeling. The reason for my C-section was her size compared to what my body could physically deliver. Healing from a C-section is not a quick recovery even when it goes well. There are physical challenges you face as you heal on top of caring for a new baby. It is considered a major surgery and there is more than the traditional postpartum care that you can do to help yourself heal. If you're having one, I highly suggest looking into what physical therapy you can do after the surgery. There are a lot of OB-GYNs that do not practice that as a standard part of care afterwards.

I never expected that the birth of our child was not going to be the hardest part of this birthing experience. A couple months after her birth, I was diagnosed with postpartum depression and anxiety. I spent the first two months having daily panic attacks. It was hard to hear so much positivity about something that should be a majorly joyous moment of my life and yet feel like I was absolutely struggling.

Without the support of my husband, I don't know that I could have gotten through it as well as I did. After much contemplation, I made the decision to start some medications, switch to formula feeding, go to counseling, and join a support group. Within a couple of months, I was feeling better. Overall, it was a two-year mental health journey.

The moments when we face huge obstacles are oftentimes the moments that give birth to something monumental in our lives. Yes, that experience was challenging, but I wouldn't change it even for a second. It led me to church and building the foundation of my faith. It brought me closer to my husband. It gave me the opportunity to be a mom to an amazing little girl. It pushed me towards building up my business more and ultimately opened the door for some pivotal moments in my career. Looking back, it was a moment that sparked the beginning of my massive healing and faith journey. Without that, I wouldn't have been as prepared for what my future was to hold.

Five years later, we found out that we were expecting our second child. By this time, I was fully grounded in my faith. God had shown up time and time again in my life. From opening up opportunities in my career, as I worked hard towards my dreams, to healing from the postpartum depression. I had learned that I didn't have to have all the answers or even the understanding. I could lay everything at His feet and let go of the weight that I carried. I could give purpose to all my experiences. I fully trusted the journey I was on.

I knew without a doubt that I would have to lean into my faith with this second child. I would have to be incredibly aware of my mental health and practice good self-care. We knew what we had experienced the first time and we had a plan to help not experience that again.

The thing about life is that things do not always go as planned. There are some moments that you can't plan for or even see coming.

About four months into my pregnancy, I got a gut feeling that our little one was going to come early. It was so strong that I didn't even question it and knew in some ways God must have been preparing my mind.

At work, I was in charge of a major conference that was relatively close to the time that I was due. As we worked on building out timelines, I knew that I had to account for her arriving early. I absolutely knew that I would not be back to work after the 4th of July. If that ended up being the case, she would be about 3.5 weeks early. Other than that strong knowing feeling, my pregnancy was relatively easy on me. I can vividly remember saying to myself that "I don't know what is fully in my future, but I know you've got this, God."

On the 4th of July, we went to our town's parade as usual. I was surprised at the fact that I wasn't dying from heat for the first time. It is always so hot at the parade. When we got home, I felt off and realized I had started bleeding. I decided to lay down for a little bit to see if maybe I just overdid it in the sun and heat. I knew I had a doctor's appointment the next morning and I had a bag packed just in case. I had been planning in case my gut intuition was right. The rest of that day, I laid on the couch at our family cookout and we went to watch fireworks that evening.

The next morning at the doctor's appointment, I realized my situation was much more concerning than I could have imagined. I was diagnosed with severe pre-eclampsia and sent directly to the high-risk maternity unit at the hospital. I was in the beginning stages of labor and my blood pressure was in dangerous stroke ranges. My stay in the high-risk unit didn't last long and I ended up having an emergency C-section the following day.

It did not go anything like the first time. In fact, the reality of our experience is that my husband came very close to losing me and our little one. When I finally fully "came to" a couple days later, I realized that physically I was not in a good place. I could look into my husband's eyes and know that what we had just been through was serious.

I had just survived stroke level blood pressures, a postpartum hemorrhage, and an overdose of the medication to prevent strokes. I vaguely remembered that our daughter had not been moving when she was born, the desperation in my husband's voice and her small cry as he did skin to skin and coaxed her along. My body was badly bruised from all the attempts at drawing blood or getting an IV to stay in. It felt like a bad dream. Then as I tried to move a little, I realized that somewhere during the process an old snowboarding injury to my back had been reinjured.

The only pain management that has worked for that injury is chiropractic care and I would have to wait eight weeks until my C-section healed to be cleared for that. That meant eight weeks until I could *start* healing my back. My vision of what my obstacles would be were blown apart. I did not have a plan for this.

We had so much to be thankful for and yet so much to overcome. Not only were we caring for a newborn baby, but we also had the healing from the C-section, managing the pre-eclampsia, helping my anemia, and managing the pain I was in. Our oldest child still needed to be loved and cared for by us. We knew how hard it was to manage my mental health with the first child, and this was so much more to carry. It only made it harder when I was told "enjoy it, it goes by fast" or "these are the best days."

The injuries to my back paired with the surgery had left me in a state where walking was extremely painful. I could barely hold our little one. I could barely walk from our bed to the kitchen. My husband became a super dad caring for us. I turned my main focus to healing. I broke my normal independent nature and asked for my parents to come help us. Our church was constantly praying for us, checking if we needed anything, bringing or offering to bring meals.

I remember breaking down one day feeling completely overwhelmed at all that I had to overcome. It felt bigger than I could carry. I felt guilty over needing so much help. Anger at not being able to help as much as I wanted. I was frustrated with my pain and how slow healing seemed to be going. Scared at what the end result of my healing would even look like. I really just wanted to hold my baby and not be in so much pain.

My husband was always there gently reminding me that I could not control what happened, but I did have control on how I moved forward. He reminded me of my strength and that nothing was too big for God. I had a choice at that moment to let my situation get the best of me OR I could lean into my faith, husband, and family in order to keep moving forward. I prayed for God to give me strength in the moments I didn't feel strong.

We can find peace in knowing we don't have to carry these burdens alone. We can find rest without having to solve it all. My healing has been tiny steps forward. Sometimes it has felt like 3 steps forward, 2 steps back. It has been forward progress, nonetheless.

My favorite scripture that has encouraged me over the years is Matthew 11:28-30. "Come to me, all you who are weary and burdened, and I will give you rest. ²⁹Take my yoke upon you and learn from me, for I am gentle and humble in heart, and you will find rest for your souls. ³⁰For my yoke is easy and my burden is light."

In the beginning, I set very small walking goals for myself. I took one day at a time getting a little bit farther in my walking distances. I forced myself to keep my eyes on the goal in front of me. We rejoiced in the moments I managed to walk to the kitchen, down the driveway, to the mailbox, across the street, a few houses down, several houses away and, finally, around the block. Trust that God will help you through it. Set small goals that you can celebrate when you reach them. Don't be afraid to ask someone you love for help. Give yourself some grace in the moments when you doubt yourself.

Healing from this life experience has been a long journey. Three years later, I'm not only walking, but I'm able to run now. I've done tremendous healing both mentally and physically. There are still things I'm trying to find answers to or heal fully. I don't wish a moment of it away because it sparked the beginning of something bigger than me and gave me a wonderful daughter. We can overcome more than we know. We just have to have faith and trust where we are heading.

ASHLEY PAUL

Ashley Paul is the owner of Finding Authenticity, Life Coach and a leader in the creative industry. Over the years, she has held several leadership roles, owned her own business, had two children, and spent time healing from trauma.

After having her second child, she realized how important living a healthy, balanced, faith-filled life was to her. She set off on a journey to heal every part of herself, embrace and fully understand herself (all the good and bad), and live authentically.

Slowly simmering in her heart for almost six years, this journey led her to realize a calling to help others realize their potential and get out of their own way, help individuals find their voice, help leaders motivate their teams, and help people overcome the fear of failure and embrace growth.

Through nearly two decades of leading and a lifetime of different mental health obstacles, she discovered that we all have the ability to change our lives. We can enrich our lives through cultivating our inner self, our relationships, and our communication skills. We have the power to be cycle breakers, create the life we want, and be brave enough to own it.

You can find her story, coaching information, and collection of resources at: www.findingauthenticity.com or follow along on Instagram @findingauthenticityblog.

Chapter 5

LONELY NIGHTS

by Brigette Gildemaster

L ife is a crazy mess! Life is dirty, gross, contaminated and a jumble of barf on the floor! We can strive for balance, perfection, and dream all we want but, in the end, it will all come out a mess. The plans will change, needs will change, the hope will change, the reason for peace will change. It can all seem hopeless even on the good days!

If you're hanging on by a thread with no grounding when everything is going smoothly, you can begin to question everything even if just one small mishap in life happens. So when a big, massive life-altering tornado hits, causing all sorts of things to begin flooding the house, leaving not one piece of yourself left to hang on to, all of your comforts taken away, and every perception you had of the world comes crashing in around you...That place, that is a dark place that not only words like hopelessness do not express, but a truly dark place deep down in your thoughts where you are completely isolated from the closest comforts you have always had and people you have always counted on now fail you.

That is the place I have been. I dragged every hope with me for years that my world would someday be perfect again, not even realizing it never was to begin with. The things I found comfort in were not sustainable through the tornados of life. I had a hard lesson to learn and the reality was I just needed to put it into words. Words that not only change my life daily, but bring me to tears in worshiping our God.

I Am Valuable

In one week's time, I packed up everything I had and left my husband after only 3 1/2 years of marriage when finding out he had sexual desires towards our, at the time, one-year-old daughter. Our eldest son was a 2 1/2-year-old surviving Tetralogy of Fallot baby, which we had been successfully navigating through the challenges of, including a drastic move, multiple month-long stays in the hospital, several life-threatening surgeries, and so much more. But this is what brought me to my end.

The moments after hearing what he had to say, his confessions and once again fake promises and empty words felt so surreal. He tried to reassure me he was safe while my head just spun with thoughts, "This is actually happening...This is real...He is telling you the truth, you have to act on it...This isn't a dream...Yes, he is telling you something that requires drastic action, you are not overreacting to what he is saying. You must leave. There is no middle ground to try and protect your daughter and stay.

I was so outwardly calm while I continued to have a civil conversation with him, feeling like I was talking to a ticking time bomb, but feeling completely safe with the one man I had become a wife to, grown into a mother with, cried with, and clung to for comfort. I even got through the night waiting for morning when he would leave for work, and I could take actual action. I was calm, but I was planning.

I knew I would call my parents first thing in the morning; I would begin looking for a place, finding out how to hide from him, get a divorce, and just RUN.

RUN, RUN, RUN...just get away from this unreal situation that was happening to me!

Everything providentially worked out very well. I found a place, had help with my divorce, had outward support like no one could ask for, but it was inward support that was lacking. My head just kept spinning and while I'm generally a very positive person, I began having what I now know are anxiety attacks that got worse over time, also leading into bouts of depression. What had happened to me shook me to the depths of my nervous system. I had two kids 11 months apart, and I was four months pregnant with our third child, whom I would later find out was another little girl. A life as a single mom with three kids under two and a half was staring me in the face. And even though my son was medically stable and doing well, he still had a hole in his neck from his tracheostomy that we were hoping would close on its own, his oxygen levels had to be monitored all night long, and more that only a mother and constant caregiver would know about in his daily care.

I did have so much support with these extra outward physical struggles especially from my family, particularly from my dad and mom, but my inner voices would just get worse – I was a failure, I could do nothing right, I was meant to struggle, I had lost perfection status, I no longer fit in with my married and family friends, but I wasn't single and "free" either. I struggled to get a grip on my new reality.

I lost friends who didn't understand or didn't know how to associate with me. People would try to say encouraging things, but it all came out meaningless and empty, if not flat out rude. I had people explain the importance of getting re-married (and soon) because I had kids and they needed a dad. Worst of all, I had people I had trusted telling me I needed to be back with my sexually perverted husband, "Is there any chance at all you could work it out with their dad?" These words still ring in my ears and I believe they are straight from the Devil.

I felt like a fish out of water, gasping for just one gulp of air, not even knowing who to trust or believe anymore, only knowing I was doing what was right for myself, my son, and my daughters.

The days of adjusting to our new home kept me busy. I had a baby to prepare for, a house to organize, a new town to explore, with friends to make and get settled into, but none of it filled that empty void of not feeling like a complete family and that something was missing. The long evenings were the worst as I continued to have my kids on a bedtime schedule and give myself quiet time. The silence was deafening. Texting friends, Facebooking®, and projects didn't keep my inner thoughts from going on and on and searching for the answer to our new life situation. "Why?," "What's it all for?" Having a spouse/partner seemed to give a bigger reason for living, a fuller picture.

Through these long nights and struggles outside of my plan, which lasted for years, I was brought into an even deeper relationship with God and His son by finally being able to grow into loving my own unique identity. Grounding myself in my own story and purpose, letting what everyone else thinks and says become an, "Oh, well. That's not for me right now" and moving on. I am firmly placed in the situation God has only given to me for His glory and continuing forward in my own beliefs. My story and purpose is not for everyone to understand.

Our God gave us the greatest gift when He sent His son Jesus to die for us. Not just because we are worthless sinners, but because He values us and we are worth the price and that price is worth paying for us to live out our stories.

When we see what God values, only then can we appreciate what He has done. We ourselves MUST also believe we are valuable. If we don't, then we will never truly understand what He has done.

Knowing and loving ourselves for who God created us to be will always give us a safe place to rest.

I believe I am special and not a failure for what was thrown my way. I was not being punished, paying the consequences for my choices or any of the trillion questions I asked myself, "What is it all for?" It's all there to fulfill God's perfect plan, not my perfect plan.

Generations of women in the Bible have their stories muddied up with scandal, deception, being *that girl*, hard choices, bravery, confidence, and more. How those women must have felt going through the moments and steps of their stories, not truly knowing how it would all end. The emotions and feelings they each must have had. Because they were all just women like you and me. Women the world would deem the most invaluable and un-put together. Yet, living out their lives, doing what they believed must be done by their own God-given convictions.

Average women were used in bringing about the coming of our perfect savior through the messiest of stories. The time was taken to tell their stories for us, because that's how important it is for us to know WE ARE VALUABLE in our messy lives. And they will be messy, but the ending will be perfect in God's plan.

A man being a pedophile is an ultimate reason to leave, and yet people said I must stay. My firm belief is that a porn addiction is enough reason to leave, a negative person is enough reason to leave, and a non-communicative partner is enough reason to leave. I've lived through it all and am on the other side seeing how it is not God glorifying to live a life with a spouse under those circumstances.

I valued myself and my children the way Christ values us by leaving my husband.

Knowing that by always seeing God's wisdom and continually searching to do the right thing I would be following His plan for me. I didn't fall into the trap of living a life less than what God had called me to. I didn't listen to the reasons of how my life needed to look perfect for others in this earthly world. I have accepted being *that woman* because what I did was God's plan for me of scandal, deception, hard choices, bravery, confidence, and doing what was right simply by believing in my own God-given convictions.

I didn't stay for the comfort of knowing tomorrow would be the same as today with my partner. I didn't stay just because I didn't know what would happen on the other side of leaving. I left, because it is how my story is going to be told.

It started by opening up to just one person I trusted, talking through my own thoughts, my own feelings, emotions, and what I thought was going on. I let them flow from me. I took that first step, getting it off of my chest in a safe space so I could think clearly through the reality of my own journey. Just saying it out loud brought healing and a clearer picture to my reality, clear back when it was *just a porn problem.*

When I first opened up to my close friend, parents, and family about our marriage issues, I gave myself a leg to stand on. It made the problems real and not made up in my head. I was able to keep searching for answers and not ignoring problems or allow him to manipulate me, as much. They gave me comfort, wisdom, prayer and helped me with creating a clearer picture of what a healthy marriage looks like.

If no one was available to talk, I used a voice recording app and re-listened to myself. It helped fill those lonely nights, work through all the thoughts, and the messiness of this new life.

Breaking the cycle, I healed and learned about myself on a deeper level. I built my confidence and impacted people around me by just being the intricately made person I was meant to be.

I've stood up for myself in ways I never thought possible. I had been very vocal with my son's medical care, but I never had to create boundaries for myself. I never thought I deserved to be respected by others, only that I should respect others. I found grounding in my decision-making. I've worked through so many emotions and sat with the pain of them; learning that ignoring it only brings others more pain, too, especially your children. I can finally trust others again and go about life without questioning the outcome.

Most importantly, I have a deeper inner-peace that I never even knew before overcoming so much.

BRIGETTE GILDEMASTER

Brigette Gildemaster began her journey of helping others with eating habits and a healthy lifestyle. She is a certified health coach and owner of The B. Wild Life, offering herbs and tinctures to help people with the natural nutrition and medicine God gave us. Because of her own personal story, she specializes in stress and anxiety, illness, and children's remedies. She is always continuing her studies: currently to be a crystal healing practitioner and in energy work.

Through Brigette's life-altering experiences, she has found a passion to help others through their unexpected life changes. She is an impactful author and a keynote speaker for many audiences both in person and virtually, making every effort to help women walk through the transition of finding out who they are now and how to let go of old dreams that aren't serving them anymore after a life-altering experience; while handling triggers that make us fear the future and, most importantly, she wants all women to be comfortable in their identity and value who they are even when they feel broken and lost in their situations.

Brigette inspires audiences to work through the aftermath of unexpected life changes by finding grounding in their beliefs, working through the past, building self-esteem from broken trust, and creating peace.

Connect with Brigette, check out her blog and podcasting episodes, and book her for your next event at www.brigettegildemaster.com.

Chapter 6

LIFE IS WONDERFULLY BEAUTIFUL

by Cathy Sever

Family has always been very important to me. I'm the youngest of seven and, as much as I know that my family has always loved me, there were many challenges growing up. I was raised in an alcoholic environment filled with lots of chaos and neglect. Additionally, throughout my childhood, I was subject to ongoing bullying. But the worst part of my childhood was when one of my sisters was diagnosed with bone cancer and passed away at the age of 11. I was only 5. My sister's illness and death crushed my family and me. I suffered from grief and separation for many years. It wasn't until I was an adult that I learned how to process my own grief.

In the years that followed, I fell in love with a kind and loving soul who nourished me with tenderness. Our plan was to get married and we had a beautiful daughter together, but he succumbed to alcoholism. After nearly a decade of trying to make things work with an absent alcoholic, it took a tremendous amount of strength and moving 1,200 miles away to finally end things.

At that point in my life, I had seen too many examples of relationships and marriages that obviously weren't working, and I was determined not to become a member of the bad marriage club. I was a young, dedicated single mother, and eager to create a happy, fulfilling life for my daughter and me. I was certain that when I married, it would be healthy, supportive, and strong, and would stand the test of time. I wish I could tell you that is what happened.

I wasn't looking to get married at the time, yet I remember feeling pretty lucky that I had found such a catch. Initially, I felt no attraction or spark – but things between us progressed quickly. He was charming, engaging, humble, and kind. He was eager to live a happy life and nurture a wonderful family. The deep, engaging conversations flowed easily between us. We discussed the challenges we faced so far in life. We shared the same values and we made a great, cohesive team. He professed that he wanted to be a father to my child, and the two appeared to get along well. He was unlike anyone I had ever met. In fact, my girlfriends referred to him as "Mr. Wonderful." He really was wonderful and it would have been hard for me to not love him. I remember thinking he seemed like a dream come true. It wasn't until after we were married that he disclosed how abusive and traumatic his childhood was. And it was after we got married that I began to see his dysfunction unravel.

Everything changed with him from the moment I said, "I do," but it didn't change all at once; it was more of a slow cook. His good qualities such as his charismatic charm and kindness became qualities reserved for when out in public, but behind closed doors at home, he was abusive, and displayed symptoms of bipolar with manic episodes. Each day became worse. Each day I felt more shocked realizing that the life I thought I jumped into was fake, while the reality was a living nightmare. Bit by bit and day by day, the qualities and person I thought he was were replaced by a dark, agitated, cold, argumentative stranger. I watched the big energy highs and lows. He would talk extremely fast and have huge energy bursts, restlessness, and stay up all night. Whenever he was like this, I became more frightened by his fast, jerking movements and those were the good days. Sometimes, he would "accidentally" push into me or bump me, so I tried my best to stay out of his way. Then he would crash and sink into deep lows that would last for weeks and months where he would seldom do anything but go to work and come home and go to bed. While in his depressed state, he rarely ate and he didn't take care of his basic grooming. I urged him to get help, but my suggestion only made him angry. I kept thinking he would snap out of his bad mood and return to the wonderful man he was before we got married. Inside, I kept excusing his behavior and I kept trying to figure out how I could make things better.

Within our first three years, we had two daughters together and it was also during that time that I became depressed. Never in life have I experienced so much loneliness and felt so sick as I did in my marriage with him. It was shocking to come to the realization that the compassionate, kind, loving person that I chose to spend the rest of my life with was actually a cold, cruel con-artist.

I left in our ninth year of marriage. The hardest part was actually making the decision to leave because I felt so confused and afraid and life felt hopeless. I promised to love and cherish until death and that is what I fully intended to do. Yet children deserve safety and nowhere in our marriage vows did it state that I must promise to love, honor and live subject to ongoing abuse. The abuse had gotten so bad that I felt certain he was going to kill me and I had no idea what he intended to do with the children.

The deciding factor to leave was the children. I knew that the abuse they experienced already had long-lasting damaging effects, but if the children grew up with abuse, it would become their "normal" and they would likely find themselves in similar situations as adults. I had to leave for their safety but also to save their future lives even though I had absolutely no idea how we were going to get out safely.

I've heard people say things like, "If she stays in an abusive relationship, she deserves it." That toxic thinking is false and it's one way to keep the cycle of abuse active so I'd like to obliterate that way of thinking altogether. Relationships are not that simple; they're complex, especially the insidious nature of abusive relationships. No person can understand without actually living through the horrific experience.

I couldn't figure out how to get out safely, but I felt compelled to take action. So my primary goal beyond our safety became my own healing. I remember hearing somewhere, "Go within or go without." I learned to meditate and I made meditation a daily practice. I read every self-help book and took every course I could get my hands on and sought out alternative healing.

Eventually and unexpectedly a way out presented itself and unfolded over a course of several days during more abusive events. The children and I got out of the house safely and we visited the battered women's shelter (a place I had visited frequently over the years for support and advice). While there, I was encouraged to really listen to the story I was telling them about the life I was living. It helped me see clearly and realize this was the opportunity to get out safely that I had been praying for.

If you think living with an abuser is hard; leaving was like jumping from a burning building into a sinking ship. Every step felt completely dangerous and impossible.

But I learned that even the things that may seem impossible can become possible. I learned how the act of making one decision can bring about wonderful, even miraculous opportunities that otherwise wouldn't be available. And each time I would take a step in the direction I wanted to go, something new and wonderful would present itself. I learned that I had more strength in myself than I ever thought possible to keep moving forward on the path of healing and in the direction of my dreams.

Each day since then I have been tremendously grateful that we got out. Each day since then has been a blessing and a day of healing for the children and me. The changes brought on by separation and divorce were positive and significant.

Seven years after the divorce, I thought I had everything on track in my life. But then, life has a way of introducing its own agenda. I received a phone call that began with "Cathy, did you hear?" I was not prepared for the devastating impact that call would have on my family and me.

The call came in on a late Tuesday afternoon informing me that my daughter was involved in a car accident, and was flown by helicopter to the local ICU trauma unit. Being taken by helicopter to the ICU trauma unit sounded devastating. And it was. I grabbed my two youngest daughters and we drove 2 1/2 hours north to the hospital where my precious daughter was having her first surgery and fighting for her life.

At the time of the accident, she never lost consciousness. After the van rolled several times and she was ejected from the front passenger's window, she flew through the air about 50 feet over a barbed wire fence and landed on flat ground near a huge pile of boulders.

When I met with the neurologist, he told me in his soothing voice that my daughter would not make it through the night; she had too many major injuries. And, if by some miracle she did make it through the night, she wouldn't survive the dozen or so surgeries she would have to face in an attempt to heal her broken body. And, if by some additional miracle, she was to survive the surgeries, the best-case scenario is that she would be paralyzed for life.

In the beginning, my daughter could only move her eyes and her mouth. If her nose itched, she was dependent upon someone to scratch it. I helplessly watched my precious daughter constantly crying out for more pain meds. I saw the girl that I birthed, raised, and love dearly, swollen beyond recognition following a horrendous 17-hour surgery. I sat next to her for countless hours holding her hand, and shoveling ice chips, one at a time, into her mouth. I fought with doctors and nurses, as I screamed and demanded her rights and that they take better care of her. I begged and pleaded for mercy, and I also thanked the medical staff and I thanked God that she was alive.

My neighbor once said, "What I would give to push my daughter around in a wheelchair; instead, I visit her grave."

Surviving that horrible accident was a miracle. Surviving that horrible accident without brain injury was a miracle. Surviving nearly a dozen surgeries over a few weeks was a miracle. More than a dozen physicians were assigned to my daughter and everyone believed she would die. As one doctor put it, "I cannot explain why your daughter is here today."

During her time in critical care ICU, I lived outside myself. I felt stunned. It would be impossible to put to words the tremendous pain I felt. Even the air hurt.

My daughter is a single mother, and at that time, her three boys were between the ages of 4 and 10. The boys came to live with me and my two youngest daughters. Not only was I hurting, but so were my three girls and my three newly adopted baby boys. Once again, I needed strength to push forward and help my family pull through. It's been 15 years since the accident. The boys are all grown up. My daughter continues to progress and she says that she will walk again and I believe she will.

I cannot say that my life has been easy. I can say that I have a strong and deep love for my beautiful family and for life. The traumas and hardships I survived have brought about accelerated learning and more compassion for myself and others and I'm a better person because of it. Sometimes life can fall apart, but it's not to crush us; it's to open and expand us. Pain has a way of bringing you to your knees to go within and ask deep questions. I've learned that anchoring and grounding myself deep within has enabled me to draw upon strength at levels I never thought possible, and become more resilient and open-hearted so that I can weather through anything while I create the life I deeply and truly want and desire.

I hope that by sharing my story, women will feel less alone and have faith in believing that there's always a way through; you're stronger than you know. I hope you realize that you can do anything and I hope you know how loved and worthy you are and life is supposed to be good and can be good for you and for me.

I have so many things that I am grateful for. Life is wonderfully beautiful.

CATHY SEVER

Cathy Sever is an international best-selling author, transformational coach, and an inspiring speaker. Cathy is fiercely committed to sharing the powerful lessons she has learned in life to inspire audiences and help empower heart-centered women entrepreneurs to get unstuck and step into satisfying, purposeful, successful lives.

Cathy can be reached at cathysever@mail.com.

Chapter 7

FAITH, FAMILY AND FIGURING IT OUT

by Cristy Heck

It was 2018 and my husband, Wallace, and I were walking through a very tough season emotionally, financially, and with our business. We finally felt like we could see the light at the end of the tunnel, but we were still struggling. We had begun spending our spare time at our place in Orange Beach, Alabama (OBA). It was a restorative place for us at a time when we needed it. A friend introduced us to a particularly irreverent part music, part stand-up comedy act that is a regular at the world-famous Flora-Bama. I am not sure I have ever laughed this hard, and it was a much-needed release for both of us. This was the beginning of our love affair with this very special place and it began our journey to friendships that would forever change our lives.

One hot, sweaty, standing room only, summer night, a deep and meaningful conversation began with this beautiful woman, Jamie, over the loud music and inappropriate jokes from the stage. She commented that she could not believe she was sharing so much; we had such a deep connection. It felt like we had known each other forever but had lost touch and finally reconnected. I now know this was God leading me.

Fast forward to September and a Facebook® post from a childhood friend that called me to action. I was 49 years old, overweight, terribly unhappy with myself, and struggling with my health. My stress level was incredibly high. I was searching and longing to find a place where I belonged spiritually. I was raised Catholic but, after being divorced twice, I was not very high on the welcome list. I loved the traditions of mass, but yearned for so much more connection and understanding about the bible. I needed clarity.

As my friendship with Jamie grew, I attended her yoga class when I was in OBA. We had insightful conversations, lunches with the guys, and she introduced us to "her people." I always said, "I don't like women; they are mean." My only girlfriends were my sisters. However, we both kept reaching out and Jamie kept introducing us to people "we need to know." She has created this amazing group of humans around her who cheer for one another, love one another, do battle FOR one another, and protect one another in a way I have never experienced. There are NO mean girls! As our friendship deepened, and my life began to change, my marriage began to change.

I was turning 50 and that social media post that called me to action was what I believed I needed. So, I scheduled a call, and took a leap of faith, again, led by God. It had to be God because all the things I needed to do for success in this program were things that had been non-negotiables in my life prior to this. I yearned to be healthy, and to feel like me again, but had no idea how to get there on my own. This is where my life took such an unexpected journey, one I could not have imagined in my WILDEST dreams. God took over, and I leaned in.

He brought me to Jen Jones's "Significant" online course, which put me on a Zoom® call with 25 women talking about faith, family, and business for six weeks. He led me to build my relationship with Jamie and trust all the people she introduced us to. He called me to attend Brooke Thomas' live event with 50 women I had never met to learn more about faith, business, and women who support and help each other. All of this was being laid out in front of me, and there was NO hesitation to attend, only encouragement. I was terrified and awkward every time. However, God met me there. I did not realize at the time, but the right people, saying the right things to me, continued to show up every time I was about to falter, fail, or cancel. I was so intrigued, yet overwhelmed, with this new faith, these conversations with God and with other women.

Along this journey, I lost 30 pounds and found a very healthy me that had been hidden, not only beneath layers of fat, but habits that no longer served me, a faith that was lacking, and a soul that had become hardened towards God. I had been completely lost and my health journey was uncovering more of my heart and faith than I could possibly have imagined.

My husband had a heart attack in December of 2019. While I was finding my health, he was struggling with his and stress was literally killing him. He made the abrupt decision to sell the family business. Understanding the magnitude of this decision is important. Monumental is an understatement. It was a second-generation family business heading to the third generation. We worked every day with our sons, just as Wallace had with his father. This business was 63 years old. His decision to sell his legacy is only explained by God, which led us to the next step.

We have a huge, blended family, and they are our world. Family dinners are important; 25 or more is the norm. Our home was a revolving door of kids, grandchildren, family, and friends coming in and out every day, like a bed and breakfast. Our mothers live down the street, and my grandmothers live within two miles. Every family event and every holiday were hosted at our home in Baton Rouge. Weddings, showers, announcement parties, birthday parties, graduation parties, welcome home, and going away parties, all at our home. There were times when family seemed more like business, but it was the life Wallace and I had created together, and it was ours. Selling the business had changed so much in our family relationships, especially with our sons, but we were figuring it out, until God threw us a new curve.

We were both so drawn to the friendships we had made and the life we were creating in OBA that we sold our home in Baton Rouge. It is our version of starting over with God as our co-pilot making choices that are right for us, based on His guidance with people who brought out the best in us. It was awkward and uncomfortable in many ways, but so very right in others. We were becoming more aware that God had a plan, and we needed to listen.

Friends, community, feeling like you belong, learning to listen to God and ask for direction, life was changing so much and so fast. I was in awe, with a childlike wonder, still a little bit terrified. We had this new life, new friends, living at the beach, no home in Baton Rouge, and changing family dynamics. It was all so strange, yet felt so good. It was like going off to college and leaving your family, but we were adults, with grown children, grandchildren, and responsibilities. It was surreal, but we were creating our new life.

In August, Angie, a friend that Jamie introduced us to, who was in end stage kidney failure and on dialysis, was finally approved for the kidney transplant list. I never hesitated when she shared the information on how to be tested. My first conversation with Ochsner Multiorgan Transplant unit was so long and after reading through the materials and answering the questions, I was approved to do blood tests.

My husband's reaction was NOT what I expected. He expressed tremendous concern for me, my health, our life. It was hard for me to understand his reaction because his father was a kidney recipient. His best friend was a kidney recipient with his wife the donor, and they had five children at home. What on earth did I have to be concerned about? I was healthier now than any other time in my life. My faith was stronger, and I was surrounded by friends who loved and cared for me. What was the problem? What could go wrong? It took lots of prayers and conversation, but Wallace supported me with getting tested, and we would cross the next bridge if it came.

I scheduled the appointment and was told it would take two weeks to get results. It was only 10 days when they called and told me I was a match. Here was the next bridge, and Wallace was not ready. I prayed, and God did His thing. I explained to Wallace that I really felt called to do this. I would not have been a match if this were not God's plan. It was important to me to continue to the journey and see where it led. Wallace loves me and supports me; however, he was concerned.

I waited to tell Angie in person. As we were walking the trails in Gulf Shores, we discussed the fact that her brother was a match, but could not meet the strict requirements necessary to go through further testing for donation. As we walked briskly, I told her Ochsner confirmed I was a match. The absolute shock and joy that filled her face is something that is engrained in my heart forever. Our journey began.

In the months that followed, there were massive amounts of blood work, medical testing, retesting, family histories, and gathering of medical records. If there was a nodule out of place from my throat to my knees, I would know about it, and get checked out. Once all of this was done, the transplant panel review meeting was required. This testing went on for months. On December 14th, we were finally both approved for transplant, and our surgery was scheduled for February 7th.

The first real understanding of the impact this would have on our friends came after dinner one evening. Our friends, Grant and Tara, were the last to leave. We were all walking down the hall and Wallace casually mentioned I was a match and we had been approved for surgery. I will never forget Grant's reaction. He hugged me so tight and cried, it took his breath away. He told me thank you for saving his friend's life and how much he loved us. This was truly the first time I ever thought about how worried all our friends were for Angie. You see, from the first blood test, I never doubted what I was supposed to do. I knew God had us, and it was all going to be fine. This was when I realized how deep these friendships were and why God had put us here with these people.

We had already planned a trip to Hawaii for January, and Angie was able to arrange local dialysis while there so they could join us. On our last night, our friend Jeff (another Jamie introduction) was quiet. Suddenly, he stood up and said that God had really been working on his heart, and he had been thinking a lot about what was going to happen when we returned from vacation. Angie and I were having surgery for the transplant, and Tara was having her final breast reconstruction revision after her double mastectomy. Glass of wine in hand, among friends, in a condo on the beach in Ko'Olina, Hawaii, among laughter, love and joy, our friend prayed the most beautiful, eloquent, heartfelt, thoughtful personal prayer for our protection, our healing, and the wisdom and strength of our physicians. It was magical. I had never experienced anything like this.

These are the special people God led us to. The kind of friends that hug you so tight and tell you they love you, the kind that will stand up during a birthday dinner to talk about friendship, love, God, and the need for us all to pray together. The kind of friends who come to New Orleans for two nights when you are having surgery even though they have been told they cannot come to the hospital. The kind of friends who break those rules and walk in like they own the place and sit with Wallace and Trip and wait the hours during surgery, so they are not alone. The kind of friends who when the doctors say, "Heck family," walk up with Wallace, and the same when they called "Hendrix family." These are the kind of friends who pray for you behind your back, that cheer for you, love you, and tell you "you geaux girl"! The kind of friends God led us to in OBA.

To quote Tammy (Jeff's wife), "God is doing a thing down here, and I want to be a part of it." God is DEFINITELY doing a thing here, with these people, and I am forever grateful to be a part of it. If I can impart any wisdom from this journey, take the leap, be obedient, listen to God with all your heart; you never know where this may lead, but I can promise you, that it will be beyond your wildest imagination!

Angie is doing amazingly well. She continues to improve with normal kidney function. She will take antirejection medication for the rest of her life, but she is doing amazing. Tara has completely healed from her surgery and is cancer free. I am all healed and training to climb Kilimanjaro in February. And to top it all off, me and the Holy Spirit are leading a bible study with a few friends. I know 100% that God has all of us, and this journey is exactly what he has planned for me, and I am so deeply grateful I took the leap, and each step that followed to get me here.

CRISTY HECK

Wife, Mom, and Lollie to a huge, blended family. She and her husband, Wallace, have 5 daughters, 4 sons, 13 grandchildren, 1 great grandchild, 2 grandchildren in heaven, and 2 grandsons on the way. They live in Orange Beach, Alabama, having recently relocated leaving all their family in South Louisiana.

Cristy attended Louisiana State University and worked in the financial services industry handling business and estate planning needs for clients for over 15 years. She left the industry to work with her husband in his second-generation family ready mix concrete business. Upon selling these operations, she began her journey to uncovering what God created her to do.

Faith, family and figuring it out is her motto. Faithfully working and learning more about the bible each day, surrounding herself with people who make her reach deeper, and listening more to what God has to say in her life. Her family is her everything. She and her husband are figuring out the move and how to make each moment with her children and grandchildren purposeful. Quality over quantity.

Recognizing the monumental importance that health played in her being able to help her friend, she now coaches others on their journey and teaches her clients to protect their most valuable asset, their HEALTH. She specializes in weight loss, nutrition, healthy movement, and uncovering the why in her clients' lives. Helping her clients become the healthiest version of themselves to be ready for what God has in store for them is her passion.

Connect with Cristy at https://www.facebook.com/cristy.heck/

Chapter 8

IT'S OKAY NOT TO BE OKAY

by Elise DeBono

To whomever is reading this, I want you to know that you are never too far gone from God that He can't change your life or circumstances. You are never too far gone to where healing can't find you. You are more than any diagnosis a doctor will give you, and you can truly overcome anything you have been through. There is magic inside of you at your very core and there is a grace that extends to you from the highest of highs. This grace comes from the one that made you in His image and knows everything about you. My journey that I share is a heavy one that is faced with mental illness and other trauma I have faced, but it is also one of overcoming and triumph over the obstacles that I once let define me. It's one of simply learning how to reshuffle the deck and play the cards that life has dealt and to use it to your advantage. To change the narrative from mentally ill to mentally skilled.

Being diagnosed with a serious mental illness at the ripe age of 21 was both life-changing and traumatic. The doctor handed me my discharge papers following a two-weeklong stay at the looney bin. I was left with a diagnosis of Severe Bipolar 1 with Psychosis and a pair of the ever-lovely grip socks they give you as a souvenir from a horrendous stay. It was like someone had taken a permanent marker to my forehead and drawn the words "crazy" in permanent ink. How could I have made it through the first twenty-one years of my life only to be staring at a life-changing diagnosis that will continue to affect me for the rest of my time on Earth. Even with periods of normal in between these cyclones of insanity, I would be faced with taking a pill every day of my life that would keep me stable enough to carry a job and take basic care of myself. My prognosis was bleak, but I was determined to overcome.

Bipolar 1 with Psychosis is defined as someone having episodes of mania or depression that involve delusions or hallucinations or false beliefs. One in five people will be diagnosed with a mental illness in their lifetime. The onset for severe mental illness is between the ages of early 20s for men and can go up to the early 30s for women. Chances are you or someone you love has walked a similar path.

So, let's talk about what led to my hospitalization. How does one go from being deemed able to live in society to suddenly a "threat to themselves and others?" This diagnosis was triggered by a stressful time in my life. My first year away at college. To paint the scene, I was a broke college student trying to work a full-time job to keep the lights on. This was all while attending the University of South Florida full time studying Biology and attempting to have a social life. I had just ended things with a college boyfriend and was struggling to make it from paycheck to paycheck where I began to feel a bit off. At first, in my room I felt the presence of angels and people that have passed on. I knew how crazy this sounded and refrained from telling my three college roommates that were rooming at the same dorm as me. I sat up and pondered this and then fell asleep. Upon waking the next morning, I felt this sudden urge to flush the Adderall® I had been prescribed for ADHD down the toilet. It felt as though something came over me and I flushed the entire bottle. These pills I later found out could have contributed to a loss with reality. I woke up the next morning and remember having this increasingly strong epiphany to call my terminally ill father and confess my love for him. I remember I had apologized for a recent conflict we had that I held off confronting and proceeded to tell him, "Dad, I don't know how to say this, but last night I felt the presence of angels." "Oh, and by the way dad, make sure you go to church this Sunday." He proceeded to tell me, "Elise, I'm an Usher at church and I will be there this Sunday." Thinking this was odd of me to say, I hung up the phone not knowing this would be the last conversation I ever had with him as he died exactly one week later. I never understood why this happened the way it did, but this chain of events led me to have more faith that someone larger than me was in control.

This became the beginning of a two-week full psychotic episode where I spent most of my time in a hospital gown and slipper socks. Some days I was allowed out of my room to wander the halls and try to converse with other patients, while other days I stayed in my room and rapped some Eminem songs because it helped to cope with the true insanity I was faced with.

After two weeks of a stronghold on the psychiatric ward, I was released into the care of my mother and to rejoin society.

Following my hospitalization, I remember my Mom taking me to the beach where I, in full clothing, jumped into the ocean without a care in the world. I felt the rush of the salt water against my skin and, as crazy as it may sound, I felt the ocean begin to heal my emotional wounds. The delusions or false thoughts stayed in my mind for another couple of weeks until they resided. My mom was my primary caregiver and helped to bathe and feed me until my mind had healed from the episode, and I began having normal thoughts again.

Following my hospital stay, I had to try to explain to my friends what had happened to me, even though I didn't know myself what had happened. I could tell I was becoming ostracized from my friend group as no one really understood what I had gone through or really cared to try to understand. The whispers became louder, and some friends left never to return again. This led to a deep depression and thoughts of suicide crept in. I came up with a loosely orchestrated plan to end my life. I remember going to therapy where I confessed to what I had planned to do and my therapist promptly intervened. He truly saved my life. I was fortunate to have had a handful of true friends to count on to get me through. They loved me without conditions and welcomed me in my off state. Some even showed up for me in the hospital when I needed them the most; this always meant the world to me.

I became so fascinated in trying to understand my genetic makeup that I changed my major from the highly paid and sought-after profession of Pharmacology to the lesser paying but highly intriguing field of Psychology. I tried so hard to find people who were success stories. I didn't want to know about people who were simply surviving mental illness, but I wanted to find people thriving with their illness. I knew if I could just find one person that shared a similar story as me, it would give me the strength to press on. Just one success story. I found a YouTube® blogger who shared her journey of psychosis. She was so relatable that it allowed me to press on. The thing about the hardest moments of your life is that they truly shape you with the level of empathy to not only want to help others around you, but to write your own survival guide for them. The thing about going through hell and staring face to face with Satan himself is that it makes you want to carry around buckets of water to extinguish the flames for the next person that has to walk your exact journey.

There is a quote by Brené Brown that has stuck with me throughout my journey which reads, "One day you will tell the story of how you overcame what you went through, and it will become someone else's survival guide." So, from my home to yours here are some things that helped me get through some tough times so that you and your loved ones can not only survive but thrive.

Never underestimate the power of direct sunlight. Set out each day to spend some time in the sun even if it's for a 20-minute walk outside. Some days following my hospitalization I would try to get outside, and it would be my greatest accomplishment for the day. That is perfectly ok sometimes.

Secondly, have a plan. Having a plan and a vision for your life is imperative with or without a mental health diagnosis. Gather pictures in a collage and make a vision board. Choose images of things you wish to accomplish in life or pictures that represent your perfect state of being. Get creative and do this with a friend. It is so fascinating to see what we come up with and can majorly help us in reaching our goals. Let's practice this. I want you to close your eyes and imagine the grandest version of yourself. Take note of what she is wearing, saying, doing. Allow yourself to envision this version of yourself and meditate on it. Now open your eyes. This is who you really are. Let go of everything getting in the way of you and your highest self.

Next, spend some time with God. Spending time with God and finding peace in His presence is something that I continuously work towards. With never ending distractions and noise in my life, I always try to spend some time unplugged each day with the Lord. Sometimes I don't have the energy to formulate a prayer, but the amazing thing about God is that He can read our hearts even when we are too tired to speak.

Don't forget to make time for those who matter the most. These are our friends and family. If I knew then what I know now about the support system I would come to find in life, it would have been a tremendous motivation for times when I just wanted to call it quits. I am glad I didn't give up so that I could enjoy the people in my life that I have now. I am blessed with amazing family, friends, and extended family that have been pivotal to my success in life and with this illness. Spending time with people who love you unconditionally and are there to support and guide you through life is key. If you do not have a support system, reach out to me or your local National Alliance on Mental Illness group. There are people who want to support you in getting the help you need and these people are imperative to your wellbeing with or without a mental illness.

Make sure you get the help of a professional. I wouldn't be here today if it wasn't for the help of an incredible Psychiatrist. Medicine is also crucial in the recovery process and can largely extend the time in between episodes. Since this first episode, I have been hospitalized two additional times. Adding medicine has doubled the length of time that I stayed hospital free. Always consult a trusted professional to get on the right dose.

"For a man thinketh in his Heart, so is he."
–Prov. 23:7

Focus on your thoughts, for your thoughts become your actions and your actions become your reality. If you only knew the power your thoughts have on your overall health, you wouldn't waste a single minute dwelling on anything that doesn't serve your highest good.

There are two things that have carried me through this illness: 1) my faith in the Lord and, 2) the unconditional love that my friends and family have shown me. Love will carry us through. May God bless you with the strength to press on no matter what obstacles you face in life; this is my wish for you.

ELISE DEBONO

Elise DeBono was born and raised in Southwest Florida and currently resides in the sunshine state. She earned her bachelor's degree in Psychology in 2012 from Florida Gulf Coast University. Her personal passion lies in helping others improve their mental health and succeed in their endeavors. Elise has spoken publicly several times about mental health at locations ranging from college campuses to mental health walks sponsored by the National Alliance on Mental Illness (NAMI). She began her public speaking journey on mental health after losing a childhood friend to suicide.

In her free time, Elise enjoys creative writing, walks with her dog Belle, and traveling with her fiancé Joseph. She enjoys learning about various cultures through traveling and trying new foods. She would like to dedicate this chapter to her loving parents Tony and Lisa. She credits her late father Tony for instilling in her a fighting spirit throughout his battle with Cancer and her mother Lisa who has shown her unconditional love while battling this illness. She would also like to thank her friends and family for sticking by her side through some of her toughest moments in her life. She welcomes anyone struggling to reach out to her via social media platforms or to contact their local NAMI office.

Call or text 988 and then the National Alliance On Mental Illness or NAMI for short hotline which is 1-800-950-NAMI (6264)

Connect with Elise at www.Facebook.com/Elise.m.debono.

Chapter 9

RISE THE TIDE

by Irene Elbie

Allow me to tell you what God has done for me...
What I found while seeking The Creator was healing for my soul, my heart, my mind, my family, my marriage. I found when you invite God to your battles, you will have His strength to become the person He knows you are.

My awakening began when my younger Brother, Abel, passed away suddenly in 2017 at the young age of 36. Realizing how damaged, estranged, and disconnected my siblings and I were, I wanted to change that. I wanted to shift my heart to peace and forgiveness for it all. I knew I did not want to die with any regret and guilt in my heart; it weighed so heavy on me.

My Brother's passing began my path to searching for a way to release all dark and destructive emotions that came along with my past and how to control my emotions when I felt rejected by other people, especially my loved ones. My eyes became fully opened to show me exactly how I did not want to be with my loved ones. His passing gave me the courage and the purpose to speak up and speak out on how and why we should strive for a Christ-like mind. We can be such horrible people to one another, if we allow ourselves to be.

After my Brother's death, I began exploring, researching, and learning about why I am the way I am. Why do I sometimes behave like a demon from hell when someone hurts or rejects me? Why is it that when my heart breaks or when my spirit feels defeated, it's always because of something or someone else? Why don't they like or love me?

I had to figure out how to release and not die with the darkness of being ignorant, bitter, unforgiving, unhealed, and having a hardened heart.

So, I did something outrageous! I quit my career to stay at home and raise my then one-year old son. This was what I wanted. However, after about two years of being at home and completely losing who I thought I was, I lost it even more. I became so envious of my new husband for what I perceived and projected what I truly felt about myself in my heart and began hating who I had become… just a stay-at-home mom. My perception of a stay-at-home mom was so skewed and toxic that, because of my toxic, bitter mindset as well as other people's beliefs, I began hating my beautiful life.

Some of the people I surrounded myself with were bitter, angry, lonely, confused, unhealed, or emotionally inept, and I was done being all that. I couldn't tell people around me about the chaos I felt was drowning me. I couldn't understand what was happening.

Why was I feeling and thinking this way? Why was I so ready to give up on my new marriage and break up my beautiful family? I felt like I was backed into a corner, until I wasn't. It was then that I saw that my projections and behaviors were not adding up to the different reactions and responses I was getting from my beloved husband. What I realized was that if my husband and I were separated it would be so much easier for the evil one to destroy what God brought together. The evil one has been distracting us this entire time. He knows whose we are, even if we don't. He knows that we are more powerful and stronger together than we will ever be apart. Looking back at it now, I can see clearly that we were both being attacked and tested.

Instead of going with what I know, I went with what I don't know.

The more I thought I knew, the more I realized I didn't know anything at all.

I had no idea that searching for an introduction to myself would lead me down the rabbit hole of the infinite ridges of my subconscious mind. Wow! What a journey subconscious mind is.

I took a leap of faith to get to know me, to get closer to our Lord and Savior, Christ Jesus, and to seek His face. I intentionally wanted to work on myself to change my state of mind, my state of being. I wanted to find my purpose!

I invested in myself for the very first time and I began sharing my story. I stepped into the unknown, with His Grace and Glory covering every word I thought, spoke, wrote, shared, empowered, inspired. I began investing in and getting to understand myself better. I no longer have the family and friends I had in my life before, but I do have some renewed family and friends still here and I do have new souls in my life that will always be family and friends.

Stepping outside of my comfort zone was terrifying. But by surrounding myself with like-minded souls, I was able to do the things I didn't want to do and my new circle held me accountable. I found some amazing role models, coaches, and mentors. I've learned that success leaves clues, so finding successful people and hanging out with them helped me to grow. I was seeking Jesus' face, and through Him the right people came to me.

When I began to change the way I looked at things, the things I looked at began to change. I never felt so grateful in my whole wretched life than the moment I remembered who I was and how thankful and grateful I am for seeking and becoming closer to God. You see, for it to be about others, it first has to be about us, so focusing on the things God was calling me to do and simply choosing to think differently changed everything. When I changed my thoughts, my life changed.

It all comes back to His Word and what we must do in order to walk in His Grace and presence. We must learn how to unconditionally love and forgive ourselves first before we can truly and gracefully love and forgive others, to do His Will.

Choosing to think differently ain't easy. All it took was doing one small or big thing and it sparked up inspiration in my heart, which activated that beautiful, divine heart to shoot up a jolt of that spark to my sleeping baby neurons that are in my computer brain. This created a new pattern within me! It completely broke existing patterns! By doing the work and being determined to change my life, I was able to start over with a new beginning of such amazing and divine experiences that our Creator opened, unlocked, and bestowed unto me. Just for little 'ol me!

Doing the work it takes to get out of your own created hell isn't easy; it's actually pretty freaking hard. Sharing the knowledge and experiences I gained from my journey took longer than I expected, but by becoming the spirit I've been searching for all this time, I easily overcame those distractions that got thrown at me on a daily basis.

I had to forgive myself and others. Forgiving others didn't mean I had to allow anyone who wronged me into my life; it simply meant that by allowing myself to let go of any resentments, bitterness, anger, hatred, all negative and dark emotions, when I chose to forgive those who trespassed against me and allowed to let those un-serving emotions go, I was finally able to free myself.

As Marianne Williamson so aptly put it:

"Our deepest fear is not that we are inadequate. Our deepest fear is that we are powerful beyond measure. It is our light, not our darkness that most frightens us. We ask ourselves, "Who am I to be brilliant, gorgeous, talented, fabulous?" Actually, who are you not to be? You are a child of God. Your playing small does not serve the world."

I have been led by the Holy Spirit to help Rise the Tides when others feel all alone in their murky waters, to share another way of being, by reminding you that what you think about, so shall it be.

IRENE ELBIE

Originally from Corpus Christi, Texas, Irene Elbie has been living in Anchorage, Alaska, for the past 23 years. Her spiritual and personal voyage began in 2017, after the sudden death of her younger brother, Abel. Everything within her changed that day. She began searching for clarity, which led her to becoming closer to The Creator, closer to her spirit, and more understanding of who and why we are.

Irene is the founder of Alaska MasterMinds + CO., LLC. She is also an Author, Speaker, Knowledge Broker, and Entrepreneur.

Irene mentors, coaches, and supports spouses and couples within the law enforcement community who are struggling in their relationships and with themselves, associated to lack of faith, trauma, trauma exposure, ptsd, and more.

She creates and offers personalized mantras (specifically catered to your very own desires and thoughts). These mantras help to spark up those neurons for new or altered thought patterns.

Irene, through her own experiences, investments, self-education, research, talents and love, shares, provides and facilitates masterclasses and workshops specific to mind, body, and soul workings.

Connect with Irene at https://linktr.ee/IreneElbie.

Chapter 10

AUTHENTICITY

by Jenifer Galvan

*You were never created to live depressed, defeated,
guilty, condemned, ashamed, or unworthy. You were
created to be victorious.*
~Joel Osteen

Authenticity comes from accepting our whole selves. The imper-
fections, great qualities, and everything in-between. I'm a con-
tributor to many things in this world – the meningitis vaccine (spinal
meningitis at thirteen months old); the Adverse Childhood Experiences scores and understanding our actions as adults when ACEs go
untreated (over a decade of physical, sexual, emotional, and mental
abuse); a cycle breaker (fourth generation of lived trauma my girls are
the first generation not experiencing this); to neuroscience (recipient
of four brain surgeries, now seizure-free); to the Alaskan Peer Support
Professional Role (wrote a 'manual,' trained over five hundred peers,
and serving on the commissioning body that regulates it). Today, I'm
my most authentic self. That wasn't always the case.

As the daughter of a Chief Petty Officer in the U.S. Navy, there
was a different set of rules when it came to how we carried ourselves.
That expectation played largely in my consideration to participate
in life since my genetics were already skewed. One side of them had
alcoholism and emotional trauma. The other brought alcoholism,

substance misuse, physical, sexual, and emotional abuse. That kind of generational family history, paired with my petit mal seizures and insane number of medications attempting to control them, horrified me. I was afraid of being so distracted from my life and predisposed like so many others to repeat my genetic generational cycle of addiction, mental illness, trauma, and abuse.

My earliest memories are being seven years old, sitting in my second story bedroom window gazing at my elementary school and playground, treetops as far as one could see, kept green and beautiful by the blue skies that blanketed my smalltown, Sedro-Woolley, Washington – begging my God to take me from this world. That's right, my earliest memories are suicidal thoughts.

Being formally educated now, I see that my young self was abused, broken, and living in fear. My educated self now sees her living a life of fear and self-preservation: quiet in the classroom, reclusive at recess, making friendships easier with adults as opposed to her peers, only to go home and be invisible to all those around her. This self-preservation would overlap two decades and be challenged by two complete strangers, at my lowest point. It would take an unexpected friendship turned courtship that began after welcoming two beautiful daughters into my life, one broken marriage, and the coin toss that landed me on my older sister's couch during the recovery wave of my first set of brain surgeries. In 2004, I met my current husband and his mother, lived through four successful brain surgeries, divorced my estranged husband, and buried my 21-year-old baby sister. Amidst all that chaos, I found the path to my superpower – authenticity.

When I met Miguel (my husband) and Patty (his amazing mama), my breakdown was fast approaching. The seizures were clustering because of increased stressors in my life, abandonment, two toddlers, college, work, and failing at it thus far. I was the problem child in my family, 25 years old, no coping skills, no emotional regulation, hating the world around me, and living in complete defeat. I will say it to my last breath, THEY are the reason I am here to speak my truth to y'all.

Two things stand out meeting Miguel: first was what should have been obvious to me, but wasn't – "You can sleep in my room. The bed has got to be more comfortable than the half-circle couch." I dismissed it, didn't take him up on it and continued to play the side show in the party house my older sister ran. The second time was way more obvious. My dad and his wife stayed at my bedside in shifts when I was hospitalized, making sure I wasn't alone. My sister, egg donor, and their entourage of flying monkeys showed up for attendance purposes only. Miguel came separate and spoke to me like a woman in a rough situation. He honored my dad, looked him in the eye, shook his hand and introduced himself. Dad stepped away and we talked about everything. Miguel was the first person to look past my baggage and see a woman worth getting to know.

Up until then, my personal view of me was very distorted. I was stupid, even though my grades would say otherwise. I was unlovable because I didn't know what love was, specifically unconditional love. I was disposable and unwanted. I was ugly, unlikable and reminded of that daily. I was the worst, most incompetent mother known and didn't deserve the girls I brought into this world. The only identity I deserved thus far was the complacent patient and that would be confirmed by my uncle, Christmas 2012, "You weren't supposed to get this far in life, hun. We spent your childhood planning who'd be responsible for you today, not what we'd be celebrating." Let that sink in.

From Miguel, Patty's, and my life intersection in 2004 to today, there are just three significant moments that brought wake to where I currently am as a recovery storyteller. The first moment is July 2006, living seizure-free over two years, now engaged to and living with Miguel, his mom, and both my girls – active in my counseling, and working two full-time jobs (one as the Starbucks® Kiosk Manager inside a local grocer, and the other as the Foodservice Manager at my childhood summer camp about two hours away from home); I was on top of the world and nowhere near prepared for what was about to take place.

Showing up to camp, I was ecstatic – that camp held so many fond memories of my childhood (where I could just be a kid). I was not prepared for the storm that was coming when I got there. Everything I'd worked through was about to come crashing down around me. I believed I'd conquered my demons; I wasn't looking for any triggers, flashbacks, or baggage exposure, and I couldn't have been more wrong. It may sound cliché, but just like not chewing a piece of food enough before swallowing it; not processing your back story and its impact (positive or negative) on your life can cause a psychiatric choking sensation. You know, when one's thoughts are completely disheveled, you lose your ability to control your emotions and maintain focus, and the simplest tasks feel like trying to move Mount Everest by yourself? That's how I felt that summer, and it would take four short weeks to completely decompensate. From that job termination to my mental breakdown would be just four days, three that I only know because of Miguel and Patty. Just a year before we were to be wed, everything became unraveled and I began healing.

The next six years were amazing. I married my best friend, got to know his mama and learn what unconditional love really was, found my voice and calling, got a formal education, and started my career in Peer Support. Patty continuously made time for the girls separately, did dinner with all of us, and even made a point to call each of us to let us individually know how proud she was of us as her family. I'd host all the holidays and invite my family and Patty. I still love to host. Patty would arrive early and leave late while my family would show up late and leave early if they showed at all. Patty was a matriarch to our little family and gave us so much to be thankful for.

Just three days after we'd each spoken with her and made individual as well as family birthday plans for Miguel, we got a call none of us could have or would be mentally prepared for. Miguel and I had a routine. He'd call on his lunch break right on cue for me to be walking out the door to my job at an inpatient facility or class, pending the day. That day, he called in panic, complete word salad. I had to convince him to come home and let me drive to his mom's place twenty minutes away while he continued trying to call her.

As I pulled up to her home, her car was the first thing we saw and he leapt from the van before I could even stop, raced the 30 feet between the van and the house, screaming her name while pounding on the office window and front door, unable to unlock it in his distress. I unlocked the door and he bulldozed past me. As I pulled the keys from the lock, I heard him hit the floor and let out the most painstaking whale of horror I heard in my life, to that point or since. There was Patty, the space heater in front of her legs gave no impact to her cold, lifeless body. Only thing I could do was dial 911 since Miguel was in no capacity to.

Miguel and Patty were it for family in Washington; two only children. Miguel felt abandoned and I felt lost. Throughout our relationship, Miguel kept us going, the rock of peace in my chaos. I never held that role because I wasn't at the point of wellness and recovery until then, but I learned really fast how to hold him up and let her go at the same time.

Over the next four years, our lives would have many ups, downs, just trying to come to terms with why Patty couldn't be with us anymore. Meanwhile, my family would begin grooming the girls and brainwashing them. The further I stepped away from my dysfunctional role of scapegoat, the tighter their grip became. July 2016, they'd convince my 16-year-old daughter to get pregnant hoping I'd kick her out. When that didn't work, they coached her to exploit my mental health and prove my incompetence to parent due to my inability to manage the symptoms. Because of ghost apps on the girls' phones, we saw every message of encouragement, "She'll attempt. Be gone soon.

Just keep going" (referencing my suicidal ideations). It was horrifying, but gave me the strength to finally sever ties and stand alone. It would be years before my daughter and I would reconcile. I'm okay with this because I finally placed my wellness and health above anyone and anything else in my world ~ July 23, 2016 was the last time I spoke to any of them.

When I joined my agency in August 2018, I was in a different place of wellness and recovery. I was in a place of healing and insight and finally saw myself as the changemaker, cycle breaker, and warrior of hope that I am today. I destroyed the lens that kept me broken for so long. I stopped looking to please people who had no interest in my success or wellness. I quit listening to their labels and identifiers and began making my own. I began seeing all the things I overcame in my life while counting the blessings God placed in my path to help me get here; Miguel, Patty, my stepmom turned adopted mom, and my hero, my dad.

Then, I took one more leap of faith, and pitched my passion to my agency leadership team. Every step along the way, God has given me the words and let me speak without wavering. He's given me the people to build with and opportunities to pursue with minimal struggles and pushback. God has paved every step throughout my journey, placed the tools in my path, and kept me focused without question. He has been in control for the last 43 years. Today, I teach people who feel so broken by their lived experiences of pain, abuse, addiction, trauma, and mental illness; that believe the societal opinions and labels; their true value as storytellers to help others heal. Authenticity happens when you see the person God sees, and love them through His lens. Today, I do just that – for myself and those I love and serve.

JENIFER GALVAN

 Jenifer Galvan, BA, CPC-S, CPSP III, CDC I is a trauma survivor and has been in recovery for 16 years. For the last 14 years, she's worked as a peer support professional on ACT (assertive community treatment team), IOP (intensive outpatient), transitional housing, and inpatient teams, as well as manning the suicide hotline. Today, she is the Peer Support Program & Training Manager at Alaska Behavioral Health, serves on multiple committees and boards, and over the last two years has trained nearly 500 peer support professionals across the great state of Alaska. It has been her honor to serve her fellow peers and she looks forward to many future opportunities.

Connect with Jenifer at www.alaskapeers.com.

Chapter 11

FINDING UNEXPECTED PURPOSE... TOGETHER

by Jessica Madrigal

"Hey baby... did you sleep ok?," I asked. "Yeah... ok. Ya know, the same old thing. I woke up a lot," she replied with a look of weary positivity on her precious face. "I'm sorry, baby. I know this is hard," I said for the hundredth time. What else do you say to your daughter who has been fighting something she never should have had to fight?

It was a sunny morning, which made her happy, being that it rains constantly in the Pacific Northwest. She always looks for the silver lining. God built that into her. Thank God, because I don't know if I could have, with everything I had felt over the past nine months of pain she had endured.

As her mother, I knew what I had to do. I knew I had to protect her, lead her, nurture her, pray for her, wipe her tears, sit with her, and so many other roles we as mothers fill. But what you aren't ready for when your child has to endure so much pain is how helpless you feel. You can't possibly know it... unless you've experienced it. I wouldn't wish it on anyone.

My eight-year-old lively, cheerful, and faith-filled daughter was diagnosed with Connective Tissue Disorder and Hypermobility. It was thrust upon her in a moment. God does that. He throws sudden interruptions into our lives, like uninvited wrenches, but wrenches that we ultimately, if we are looking, find are the biggest blessing of our lives, our testimony, and our greatest opportunity for growth. One day she was running around infecting everyone around her with joy… and the next she was on an ER table writhing in pain and screaming while an entire team of medical professionals worked to mitigate her agony. And as I stood by helplessly, I tried to unpack the events of how she arrived there.

Four days earlier, she had just tried to get up off the couch and her leg simply popped somewhere behind her knee. Over the next few days her pain increased to a level that was uncontrollable, and no pain medication, ice, or elevation was helping. So, we brought her into the ER. Being that she was eight years old, they started with a less intense pain medication. When that didn't touch her pain, they moved further and further into what was eventually morphine. That did nothing. What a moment that was. I clearly recall standing in the ER feeling helpless, confused, exhausted, and frankly out of control, while watching from outside the door a team trying to help her. I began to pray in the hallway. I asked God to take away her pain, to heal her body that only He knew so well, to give her peace the way only He can, and to help me manage this situation with wisdom, none of which immediately happened after that prayer.

Once they realized absolutely no medication was going to work, they came to us with an option they don't use often. They said they could sedate her under supervision for a few hours and try to "reset" her brain and pain cycle. This sometimes works to stop a nervous system response and the body can calm down… but it's not an absolute that it will stop the pain. My husband and I discussed it and decided that it was a safe enough option and signed the permission document to sedate. I remember thinking… "GOD, what IS this?!? What could this possibly be?" I was so confused.

While I was pacing in the hallway and waiting through what would be the longest four hours I can ever remember, I walked by a new mother who was sitting outside her baby's room. She and her partner had come in with a baby around the same time we did. As she sat there, looking lost, crushed, and absolutely without hope, I felt the Holy Spirit tell me to pray over her.

"Hi. How are you doing?" I said. She looked up with deep, weary eyes and said, "I don't know what to do." Every mother can relate to that. "Is this your first baby?" I asked. "Yes," she said, "I am so scared." I told her that I have been there and I have been through it. She appreciated that. But then I asked her if I could pray over her. She said yes, and the prayer I prayed came completely from God. "I haven't talked to God in so long," she said, after I prayed. I told her that was ok, that He was here with her and her baby, and that she can do this. In that moment, no matter what happened with my daughter or how hard we had to fight through that moment, I knew without a doubt, that I was meant to be there in that moment for God to touch that young mother.

After a long four hours of waiting and prayer, we watched Sophia wake up. As soon as she was aware she was awake, she immediately returned to her pain cycle like it had never been interrupted at all. At this point, the team took us out into the hallway and began to describe Connective Tissue Disorder (CTD) to us. We had never heard of this. One of the better-known types of CTD is Ehler's Danlos Syndrome. They didn't know if it was EDS or another type, but they were sure it was CTD. After that, they admitted her for what would end up being four long days in the children's hospital. We learned more about CTD in four days than most people probably do in a lifetime. This was a time of discovery and testing for Sophia. She is a fighter, a warrior, and an absolute angel. I watched her fight to understand, adapt, overcome, and to ultimately turn this challenge into a victory for God. She prayed, sang worship songs, blessed others, and overcame her pain, over and over. She's an inspiration and God worked through her more during that time than I had ever seen.

Even when she was in her deepest pain, I could see God holding her. And God knew I needed that as much as she did. As mothers, we typically hold all of our own feelings at bay until we are lying in a ball of tears on our closet floor crying out to God. We must be strong for our children when they are put to the challenge, but we sometimes forget that we need to rely on God to heal us emotionally, too. God will carry us through the pain when we have to be the rock for our children. When we are weak, He is strong.

During that stay, we had long conversations with her medical team about what to expect with Sophia's path forward with CTD. What was normal, what wasn't, what could happen, and so on. The staff at that hospital were a real Godsend and have served as our anchor, even though they don't know it, through our long journey of discovery, advocacy, and trial and error, with many professionals misunderstanding her disorder.

Her knee pain eventually stopped after a few months. She was in physical therapy for CTD specifically and had the most amazing physical therapist. We were blessed with several providers and specialists that gave her outstanding treatment and care. Over the next couple of years, Sophia would go through multiple pain cycles affecting different parts of her body. With CTD, pain cycles start and stop suddenly. Through therapy, we all learned that with CTD she would experience things like popping of joints, which her body would register as "injuries," and then she would have pain much greater than that of a typical person. She learned how to respond to the pain and eventually manage and even prevent it.

Then came the next round of unexplained pain. These were joint and connective tissue triggers registering as "injuries." She started complaining of pain in her inner ears, starting with her right followed by her left. That cycle lasted three months. Of course we followed up with every specialist and only got the answer, "I can tell you what it's NOT, but not what it IS." Thus, continuing our journey of assessing and determining if something that's happening to Sophia is her CTD or something separate. When her ears suddenly stopped hurting, it was a day of celebration! She rejoiced and so did we.

And then the very next day, literally, she began to have severe chest pain. Off to another round of specialists. More poking and prodding. More uncertainty. More explaining. More advocating for my daughter. More. This chest pain lasted for nine months. NINE. Imagine nine months of chest pain comparable to the likes of angina. No one giving you answers, praying constantly, and not being able to do anything for your child except be there for them. And as you've probably realized by now, pain medication is ineffective for her. It has no effect. She's forced to find a new way to cope.

And here is where we find ourselves where we began...on that sunny morning when I, one more time, asked my baby, "How did you sleep?" She had endured this brutal chest pain for nine months, wondering when it would ever stop, if she would always have to fight this, this way. BUT GOD. She found her deepest faith and bond with God through this pain.

Shortly after this sunny morning, Sophia experienced a miracle. It started out as a cold, and then a virus. Miracles don't always come in the package you expect them. They diagnosed her with a virus that wasn't Covid, thank God. What I hadn't mentioned before is that during this entire ordeal, she had also been simultaneously diagnosed with Vocal Cord Dysfunction and has had Asthma since she was two. So when Sophia gets sick, she stays sick for much longer than other children. We went into full treatment mode at home, staying up all night with her, running her nebulizer every couple hours, everything you do as a parent. We had a routine at this point. But nothing was working. She was coughing, wheezing, vocal cords were freaking out and causing throat vibrations, and so on. After three nights of this routine, we realized that we weren't able to keep up with her wheezing. We took her into the ER.... probably her twentieth visit up to that point. They gave her a two-hour nebulizer treatment to return her lungs to function, directed us to continue doing what we were doing, and sent us home. Keep in mind... this was all happening to her while enduring the same chest pain she had had for nine months.

Two days later, while still very sick, she went to bed as we kissed her goodnight hoping we weren't going to be up all night again. The next morning, we woke up to Sophia bounding out of her bed and proclaiming the Glory of God with joy that ALL her pain was gone! GONE! ALL of it! She had no chest pain, no cough, no throat soreness, no headache, no wheezing, and felt absolutely amazing. We spent the morning screaming Hallelujah! Praise God!! And telling everyone what had happened. That was almost two years after her initial diagnosis.

It's been a year since that day, and Sophia hasn't had one pain cycle like the ones she experienced in those first two years. She has to watch her joints and use what she learned in therapy to manage her body registering false "injuries," but she has been mostly pain free. We know this is not the end of her story with CTD by a long shot. But she has overcome like a champion through this.

Throughout this entire process, she has never passed up an opportunity to share her story of overcoming and persevering with God. When asked if God has ever brought her through anything, she shares her miracle. She feels strongly that encouraging other children that suffer from medical issues, especially, is part of her calling. She now knows without a doubt she can get through anything with God and that the miracle wasn't just the healing. It was the challenge, the journey, and the faith she was given through it all. She found purpose and triumph in her struggle. It's powerful what God can teach us through our children's testimonies.

JESSICA MADRIGAL

Jessica Madrigal is a creative digital marketer, website and graphic designer, and co-founder of Salted Orange Studios with her husband Javie Madrigal. This dynamic impact driven couple is on a mission to help Kingdom business owners discover and increase their impact. They host a weekly live devotional on Facebook® and LinkedIn® where they discuss the freedom that is found in following Jesus. Their family has followed the call of God to move across country, coast to coast, three different times. Through their experiences, challenges, and breakthroughs, they try to inspire others to believe God for bigger things and the plan that God has for them.

Together they also founded Underdog Ninja Foundation for Heart Disease that helps first responders, veterans, and their families to both prevent and live with heart disease successfully. Alongside that, they host the podcast The Heart of the Underdog where they interview people with inspiring stories of overcoming heart disease.

She and her husband have two beautiful twin daughters, who both homeschool, and live in sunny central Florida where they visit the beach as much as possible and love going to Disney and Universal all year long.

Connect with Jessica at www.saltedorange.com.

Chapter 12

HURRICANE HANKEY

by Kadie Jeweleen Hankey

I think these days it is easy to get caught up in the chaos of things. Everything happens so fast. The seasons change, kids grow up, friendships fall apart, and the world just keeps moving forward. Sometimes when I am caught up in the chaos of life, I am just desperately wishing, praying, that it will just stop; even for a moment.

I jokingly call my kids "Hurricane Hankey." It is my comic relief to the fact that I have two young toddlers moving at warp speed constantly. But I think the phrase applies pretty accurately to our life as a family. You see, our story began just three years ago.

Everything in our new family's life was moving fast, but it was so much more than just fast–paced. There was so much that was hidden, buried down deep inside our home that the outside world was sheltered from. The world saw a new love story blooming with a new baby coming quickly. They saw a fresh start and a carefree couple enjoying all the new beginnings they were encountering together. But the truth is? Sometimes it was messy. There was heartache, addiction, pain, complications, and just plain chaos.

Just a few short months before, I was trapped in a dead-end marriage. I had married young following the small-town path of graduating high school, getting married, getting a dog, settling down, and so on. But what no one told me was you really have no idea who you are or what you want out of life when you are 17. You don't understand what it really means to break toxic family cycles and you don't even know when you are caught up in them. But there I was, stuck in a vicious, dead-end cycle of going through the motions in a life I saw no way out of. It took me six years. It may not sound like that long of a period to some, but at that age? It was forever.

I wasn't looking, but out of the blue Jeremy walked into my life. At that point I still saw no end in sight to the relationship I was in. Did I fantasize about what life would be like living a life I actually wanted? Absolutely! I wanted the white picket fence, the babies, the farm out back. I wanted a husband who wanted to be home with me. A father to coach our kids' little league team and roll around on the floor with kids laughing so hard they could barely breathe. I wanted a man who wanted ME. I was stuck. But there he was. Handsome, strong, a little bit of a bad boy vibe, and for the first time in my whole life, it felt different. He had confidence and fire in his eyes. The more we talked, the more I knew everything was about to change.

Now this isn't a story about a scandalous love affair featuring infidelity, no, this was my wake-up call. For the first time in my entire life, I finally was in a place where I could openly admit I was unhappy where I was. I didn't have to be trapped in this toxic, dead-end marriage. I didn't have to settle for a man who didn't want the same things out of our life. I could actually do something about it. So I did.

In less than a week, I left my husband, quit my job, tried to move in with my mom and was then kicked out of my mom's house (her attempt at trying to get me to go "home"). With seemingly nothing left for me in the only town I've ever known, I packed my car and left. I drove across the state to one of my best friends' homes.

I didn't have the overwhelming family support that I was hoping for. My dad knew I deserved better and was in my corner. My 17-year-old sister was supportive. I had a couple friends that stood beside me. But, really, that was all. The circle of people I had grown up with didn't understand my leaving. My grandparents wanted us to work through it.

We didn't know at the time, but about this time my mom began showing signs of early onset dementia. I wanted so much for her to support me and be there for me. But, her brain just couldn't. We didn't know the dementia was even remotely involved until about two years later when her symptoms had become significantly worse. Sometimes I can't help but think that the whirlwind that was my life at that time pushed her over the edge letting her dementia take hold of her brain completely.

For the first time since I was in middle school, I looked to God. I didn't know what to say or how to feel, but I remember laying in a hammock up in the pine trees and knowing everything was going to be okay. I knew for the most part I was on my own. I had no money, no plans, no idea what the heck I was going to do now. Somehow, I knew that the Lord would carry me through this.

A few weeks later, I decided I really wanted to pursue what could be with Jeremy. We deserved a chance. Was it moving a little quick? Absolutely. But I knew I had wasted so much time just spinning my wheels being stuck in the same life and I didn't have any time to lose. I owed it to myself to put myself out there. Heck, what did I have to lose at this point?

So again, I loaded my car and I headed north to this tiny town where I knew just him. It may have only been two hours from the town I had spent my entire life, but it felt like an entirely different world. I had never lived without the support of everyone I'd ever known. I had never tried to look for a job where my mom didn't know the boss. I had no idea where to even start.

Almost all of my family and friends had completely alienated me at this point. I had blown up my life and was now pregnant with a tattooed former addict in the middle of nowhere. I still find humor in when I told my dad about him and showed him a picture, his first question was "how many tattoos does he have?" I came from a pretty conservative family. Tattoos, addiction, probation, etc. were not exactly on the list of characteristics they desired me to find in a man. I didn't get a super positive reaction from them. So, aside from Jeremy, I was pretty much on my own.

The honeymoon phase ended quickly, and things were getting HARD. We moved into a tiny apartment a short time later and, before long, we found out we were expecting our daughter. We had no money, my car had been repossessed, my pregnancy had a lot of complications and, to top it all off, Jeremy's struggle to stay on the recovery wagon had taken a turn. Things were far from a fairytale.

We spent about two years just struggling, every day. On the wagon, off the wagon. Which bills to pay before they get shut off. Two very complicated and very challenging pregnancies with babies born just a short 13 months apart. It was so hard. It was raw and it was ugly. There were a lot more downs than ups. We almost crumbled more times than I can count.

I am so grateful to the therapist I started seeing in the middle of it all. She really helped me navigate so much in a time where I was just truly lost. But we did it. We made it through some of the hardest years of our lives.

We have two beautiful, happy children and we are finally landing on our feet. How did we get there? How did this "hurricane hankey" storm of chaos finally settle and find peace? It's a simple answer really. We gave it to God.

One memorable night, Jeremy cried out to the Lord, begging him to help him overcome his addiction. To finally stop fighting just to make it another day. To give our family a fighting chance. And you know what? God answered. In that moment laying on our bed, sobbing to the Lord. He gave him peace and took away his insatiable urges. He gave him strength.

I didn't come around so easily; I had a pretty messy relationship with the big man upstairs that had left a bad taste in my mouth in middle/early high school. I truly wasn't overly excited about the whole let's go to church idea. But, I was desperate. I was so willing to do anything to help move our family through this time of pain and uncertainty. So, we went. And it changed everything.

We walked through the doors of our church, and it was surreal. The most genuine, kind people. People who didn't look at us differently and welcomed us with open arms despite our story. They gave us a home. They gave us a family we see regularly. They gave us comfort, support, and a shoulder to lean on.

Every Sunday, we just kept coming back. This church changed everything for us. They guided us, mentored us, offered support and prayer in more ways than I can even write. Our Pastor taught us the word of God and every single day our faith grew. We were baptized and married in this church about six months later. Our relationships with family mended. Our new and old friendships began to blossom. Jeremy stayed in recovery.

God's blessings showered down on us like a summer rain in the middle of a drought. We soaked it all up. It was an entirely different life for us. The answer was suddenly so clear. God will always take care of us. He will guide us and provide us with exactly what we need even if we don't understand it at the moment. Have anxiety over things that are out of your control? Pray. A car breaks down? Money is short? A kid is sick? Pray. God is always our answer. We have a motto in our house, "God will always provide." No matter what comes our way, we just turn to Him. It has healed us in so many ways. We don't have to beg for help. We don't have to suffer through things. Our father is always there.

It has been such a blessing to also be able to have our kids growing up in this newfound peace. They don't know what it was like before; they don't need to. They know now. They live in a house full of prayer, peace, and love.

Things haven't exactly been an easy ride the whole last year. Jeremy's mother passed, my mom had to be admitted into assisted living due to dementia, Jeremy was laid off, and we found out we were expecting our third child. We still don't have a perfect financial plan, and we still have struggles. Our faith is challenged by people and circumstances. But, in the end, we will always have God. And for that, we will be eternally grateful.

KADIE JEWELEEN HANKEY

Kadie Jeweleen Hankey is a woman with fire, grit and grace all wrapped up in one. She is a small-town gal with a passion for empowering women. She thrives on being surrounded by nature and animals. Kadie was raised on a farm by a mother running a small business and quickly learned the value of an honest days' work. She is a mother of three children and two dogs, a devoted wife, and a woman of Christ. Her mission in life is to share her family's journey and inspire women to take control of their life and follow God's plan for them.

By day, Kadie's works with a major cosmetic company pampering women and making them feel beautiful. Being able to be a stay-at-home mom was something Kadie never dreamed she would be blessed with being able to do. But God always provides.

Proverbs 31:25 – She is clothed with strength and dignity, and she laughs without fear of the future.

Connect with Kadie at https://www.marykay.com/kfaircloth.

Chapter 13

A BIGAMIST AND A HOVEL, A SAVING GRACE

by Kaitlin Kreczmer

"Don't let the world break me tonight
I need the strength of you by my side
Sometimes this life can be so cold
I pray you'll come and carry me home"
~Mariah Carey, Fly Like a Bird

They say that God works in mysterious ways. And while we may not always see His work as perfect Grace in the moment, in hindsight it always is.

The year was 2019 and it was a balmy spring day in Ontario, Canada. I was at the office, but my mind was adrift on cloud-9 because I had just wrapped a flirtatious lunch call with a man I was seeing. A man that I felt was becoming my boyfriend. Distracted and infatuated, I smiled and scrolled through social media instead of working. While mindlessly scrolling, I noticed an event invitation on Facebook®. The event did not capture my interest, but something else did. I enlarged the event details and my eyes were drawn to the name of someone who was tagged in the event, a name that I recognized.

It was abundantly clear that the woman who created the event had tagged her husband. Yep, you bet – the man I was seeing, my ideal man that I manifested with God, was married. It got better. His wife was the cousin of a dear friend of mine and she and I had shared some memories in my own backyard only years before. My smile faded, though I half smirked in disbelief, as I thought "uhm – what just happened?"

I spent weeks trying to process a number of feelings and emotions, including embarrassment, sadness, heartache, and I sure as hell questioned my Faith. I struggled for years with my body, my confidence, my relationships, but I was finally in a position where I loved and accepted myself, and KNEW what I wanted in a man, what I deserved in a relationship. How dare God help me to manifest…this!

My life had drastically changed in 2016 when I left my husband. The marriage no longer fulfilled me. When I married in 2014, I weighed over 250 pounds and was encroaching on a size 3x. I blamed my husband, and I blamed myself for settling into an ordinary and sedentary relationship. When I ended my marriage, I enjoyed some time getting reacquainted with myself and designing my amazing new life as a single and independent woman on a health and wellness journey.

By 2018, I was down 60 pounds and gaining confidence like a Diva! For a brief moment, I had myself convinced that I was in control of my life. I had a new body, a job, an apartment, friends and family, and now I was dating a man who checked all the boxes. Everything was aligning. Amen, I thought. It's finally my time.

I met this man at the end of January 2019. Although our relationship was only 6 weeks in when I discovered he was married, there are two things that I want to be clear on:

1. "I'm OK being lied to at the early stages of my relationship," said no woman ever.
2. That is how intimate our dates were and how attentive he was. There was no indication that he was hiding another life. The amount of time we spent together actually suggested otherwise.

Ok, you're probably wondering "how did this happen? Details, please!"

There are so many layers to this story and as much as I would love to divulge all of the scandalous details, for the sake of time I won't. But I will disclose that before I met my dream man, I had been trusted with the knowledge that my friend's cousin had recently married a man from another province and that man was a bigamist. He met my friend's cousin online and claimed to have moved to Ontario to be with her. However, her family highly suspected there was no love and he was still scheming. At the time, my thought was WOW! How could this woman be so blind? And stupid? To let a con-artist, a master manipulator and a narcissist in to her home and think it was love?

HA! Foolish of me to think that. With all of my life and dating experience, never did I think I would find myself in a similar position, let alone literally dating the same bigamist. But, considering this man's career in deceit, I felt good at least knowing that my instincts weren't necessarily out of whack. This man was just a whole new level I'd never before encountered. It was easy to be drawn in.

Being an honest individual, after I found out and rationalized the situation for myself, I decided to inform his wife of what transpired. Some might find this brazen or think that I was seeking trouble, but I wanted the opportunity to speak with her, woman to woman. It was important for her to make an informed decision about her future based on facts. Although she seemingly ignored concerns from her family, I had personal testimony that he had not changed his ways. How could that be ignored? I suspected that I was not the only one he was dating, and this was a step I could take to prevent him from further betraying his wife and other women.

What I thought might connect us as women and maybe, just maybe, result in gratitude from her, only resulted in regret for me. Believe me she did not. I'm unsure if it was anger, disbelief, desperation, or a combination, but she concluded that I was a homewrecker who intentionally seduced her husband to break up their marriage. To be very clear, I met him on a dating site and his profile said "actively seeking a relationship." There was zero seduction involved. As I understand, they are still married.

Through the days and weeks that followed, I continued to dissect every moment he and I shared together. I literally wrote a list, in chronological order, of all of our dates. I scrolled through messages and tried desperately to piece together any warning signs that I missed. I could not pinpoint anything. To this day, I have all social media content, photos, my chronological list, essentially, a plethora of evidence to provide a play-by-play of the drama. No, I'm not obsessing over the past. One thing I've learnt working in the legal field is to always cover your ass. You never know when something will resurface and it's best to be prepared. It's also been suggested by a few who know the situation in its entirety that I write a memoir, and that would be best detailed by holding on to the details.

Gossip is something I've always tried to remove myself from. I'm a private individual in that I only share certain aspects of my life and only with certain individuals. Having relationships with people who gossip is always bad news bears. For that reason, I've removed several people from my life over the years. Despite that, I found myself at the centre of a gossip chain as a result of this relationship. One thing worse than feeling totally embarrassed and gutted after giving your heart is living in a community where gossip burns like a dry summer wildfire. What did people know about the situation? What did people know about me? What were *they*, the happy couple, saying about me? I'm not one to toss around the word anxiety, but there were too many unanswered questions at once and I grew anxious with the gossip.

While simultaneously coping with that situation, I was working my way through a private family matter that left me feeling angry and ostracized, putting a wrench in the close relationship I had with my mom. The weight of everything that was *happening to me* was much too much and it broke me, crushing me to my knees. I crumpled in to deep depression and my bubbly personality dissipated. I decided my new life was not amazing after all. In reality, my apartment was a decrepit basement hole I dubbed 'the Hovel,' I was employed in a position I begrudgingly held because it paid the bills. I earned enough money to maintain a mundane pay-cheque-to-pay-cheque life and I could hardly afford the high price of Ontario hydro. Toques, blankets, and sweaters were frequented in the Hovel year-round. I had officially hit the lowest of lows and I was done. Everybody in my life was growing and achieving and I had the Hovel, a bigamist, and was at the center of a gossip chain.

I became Jekyll and Hyde. In the presence of others, life was fine, I was happy and joyful. When I was alone in the Hovel, and sometimes before I even made it inside, I cried, that ugly, hyperventilating cry. With blurry eyes, I would stumble down the gloomy stairs of my building and make my way in for a bath. I would struggle from my clothes and then submerge myself in water that was perfectly warm and meant to soothe. The water only intensified my depression and I would ask, no beg, for God to take me, let me die. As I sat in the tub, I used my fingernails to mock the running of a blade across my wrist. I pressed just hard enough to leave red marks and scratches. I also attempted to drown myself. I'd lay in the tub with a glass of wine, which should also soothe the soul, and attempt to submerge my face under the water. It never worked. I think because the Hovel was only equipped with a shallow, broke ass tub and I could never actually get both my nose and mouth under water. The catatonic routine carried through the spring and summer of 2019, but by Fall my darkness was the only thing that drowned, and a tide brought in a beautiful light.

"Weeping may endure for a night, but joy cometh in the morning" – Psalm 30:5

It was the most ironic thing that lifted me from my catatonic state. When all the rumours about my relationship had surfaced, I received incredible support from my family and friends. I also received support from the family of my boyfriend's wife. Given their suspicions of his character and facts they learned of this past, they found my version of events to be credible and expressed sympathy for the way I had been treated.

At one point, an aunt within their family said to me, "the world needs more women like you." I didn't think much of it at the time, but those seven words became the bright light that saved me. That, ladies, was my message from God. The world needed me, women needed me, my family needed me, and I needed me to step up and redirect the course of my life. And that is what I did. I quit my job and in 2020 I scooped up my cats and belongings from the Hovel and started the new year in a bigger city. Despite years of poor self-esteem and having myself convinced that I was an introvert, I secretly knew I had a personality and charismatic energy that exceeded the boundaries of a small city.

There is a reason I didn't drown in this experience. God's vision for me was bigger than that broke-ass tub. What I experienced was a divine intervention that emancipated me from all past-insecurities and propelled me towards my best life. What I thought was happening to me was happening for me. Obviously, my preference would have been to have not dealt with that shit at all. But God doesn't always listen to our preferences. If I hadn't learnt to let go mentally before letting go physically, I wouldn't be here now.

Since my emancipation, I've become more grateful for this beautiful experience called life. For the first time ever, I'm living free from fear of judgment and have worked past my self-worth issues. I've gone on to lose a total of 100 pounds and I radiate Diva-like confidence. I'm genuinely happy and my joy is not a façade.

So, there it is, in writing, the truth. My truth about how my insecurities and mistrust led to suicide, but how I survived to thrive and help other women with their worth. You are not defined by bad relationships or gossip. You are defined by your thoughts and reactions. Align with your highest good and let God handle the rest.

MS. KRECZMER

Ms. Kreczmer is 36 years old and currently resides in Ottawa, Ontario. She is well educated, having her Bachelor of Education diploma, Honors Bachelor of Arts diploma, and a Human Resources Certificate. Having entered a new chapter in her life with refreshed confidence, she is a serial entrepreneur, solely focused on her mission to help other women develop positive body image beliefs and live each day fiercely, powerfully and unconventionally care-free. Ms. Kreczmer is a body image and mindset coach, specializing in self-worth and confidence. Most recently, she founded Master Your Body – Mindset Coaching where she elevates and empowers women to live their best lives NOW. She has designed custom coaching programs that work to transform mind and body and developed the MYBody Badge for her clients.

As part of her mission and to reclaim years of lost style personality, Ms. Kreczmer founded Bohemian Beach Boutique, a fashion boutique that advocates for women with Bohemian inspired fashion and beachwear that evokes confidence. Ms. Kreczmer aims to prove that fashion can be blind to prejudice and that summer is meant for every body. In her spare time, Ms. Kreczmer can be found in her kitchen, at the beach, hiking, traveling, reading, writing, or shopping. At the end of long days, she finds solace in sipping wine in her soaker tub. Yes, she is still single.

Connect with Ms. Kreczmer at https://linktr.ee/mybodymindsetcoaching.

Chapter 14

OVERCOMING RESILIENCE

by Karsta Hurd

"Wow, you've really overcome a lot [of experiences] in your life." By some definitions, yes. But, I don't believe we overcome difficult experiences. Rather, we overcome the limiting beliefs that are the byproduct of those experiences. I didn't overcome the experience of having an abusive, alcoholic father. I endured that. I overcame the belief that I didn't matter. I didn't overcome being sexually abused at the age of eight. I overcame the beliefs that my voice didn't matter, that it was better to keep quiet so as not to upset anyone and that my body was the only way to get attention from men. I didn't overcome a bad marriage. I overcame the belief that that's all I deserved. So no, I haven't overcome a lot of experiences. I've survived a lot of bad experiences. Now I'm working hard to overcome the limiting stories and beliefs I carry because of those experiences.

For as long as I can remember, people have described me with words like resilient, strong, independent, warrior. And, while I know that many see those as admirable qualities, it never quite sits right with me. I don't want to be resilient. Resilience highlights the struggles I've endured. And in order to continue being considered resilient, it requires the endurance of more struggle (at least that's what I've always felt). Quite frankly, I'm tired of enduring struggle. My entire life has been one long marathon of enduring struggle. So, I'm done surviving. I'm ready to overcome and thrive.

It should be no surprise that growing up in a relatively constant state of survival, one becomes quite an expert at certain skills: how to keep quiet, how to take care of one's own needs, and how to keep one's expectations to a minimum. In addition to that, I became an expert in settling for anything that maintained balance. I learned to accept things that were "fine" because it was better than "not fine." I was, for all intents and purposes, grateful for "fine." I was so grateful for "fine" that it became the standard I aimed for. Even when my soul was screaming at me to be brave and try something extraordinary. "Fine" was always good enough.

During my third year of college, I had a vision, a God wink if you will, of becoming a successful international businesswoman. I could see, actually I could feel what it would be like to travel the world on private jets, wearing designer clothes, and being extremely powerful and independent. It was so exciting! It was also so far beyond "fine," a fact I was quickly reminded of when I barely passed Accounting 101. In the spirit of being grateful for what I had, I declared a major in education and graduated with my teaching degree. After college, despite *multiple* signs that I shouldn't, I got engaged and married to my college sweetheart (I'm not exaggerating when I say that I wanted to break off the engagement at least three times-once on the actual wedding day). I had a good job, we built a perfect picket fence life in the suburbs with a dog, two beautiful children, and even got a minivan. And it was all…. Fine.

There's nothing particularly wrong with "fine" – in some instances, fine is all we have. But when you've curated an entire life full of "fine," you spend much of your precious time and energy maintaining relationships and experiences that don't give much in return that it ends up being pretty exhausting. And I was—exhausted. Every ounce of energy I had went into juggling and maintaining things that in my soul I didn't want.

The Universe (God, Source, Creator) tried warning me. She sent me nudges, niggles, and intuitive hits at every turn. Much like the vision in college, she would show me what could be. I could feel the potential for greatness. Often, those visions didn't make sense. Sometimes they were downright scary (in the best way). Since I hadn't yet overcome all of the limiting beliefs from my childhood, I continued settling for "fine" well into my 40s. The thing with the Universe is that she's a little like a toddler sometimes. She'll ask for your attention through some kind of intuitive nudge, perhaps butterflies in your stomach when you're headed for something amazing, or a sinking feeling in your chest when you're headed in the wrong direction. It's quiet, almost a whisper. If you don't listen (like I didn't), she'll start yelling at you a little louder. She'll perhaps throw an obstacle or challenge in your way, or send you visions of greatness that seems just a little too unrealistic (but amazing). And, if you still don't listen, she will start having a full-blown temper tantrum, basically sending a freight train to demolish your life so that you are forced to start over.

That's what happened to me. After decades of ignoring every sign, signal and vision she sent me; building an entire life that was not intended for me, piece by piece it came crumbling down. It was gradual. Which in a lot of ways made it even more challenging. It felt like one bad thing after another was happening to me. It was like reliving my childhood. I added a new limiting belief that I was just somehow destined to spend my life suffering. Besides, I was resilient, right? I was made for struggle.

Eventually, everything I had curated and endured since I was 22 years old was gone. And, in 2018, I decided it was time to start rebuilding.

If you've ever watched a home improvement show on HGTV®, the process was a lot like that. Every time I knocked down one metaphorical wall, more (emotional) damage was exposed. Until eventually everything was exposed, all the way down to the studs. I left my career of more than 20 years, and a second long-term relationship ended. I was working random part-time jobs (that didn't even cover half of my monthly bills) while I tried starting my own online coaching business (which I had no idea how to do). Like home renovation, this process took twice as long, required twice as much energy, and cost twice as much money as I expected. My expertise in resilience and strength served me well in enduring the challenges, but my lack of experience in dreaming, planning, and thriving made this renovation extremely difficult at times. Even in the darkest moments, I remained steadfast in my dedication to following my heart. Because the most important lesson I've learned through all of it is that my intuition is my greatest strength. This time around, the nudges and God winks would not be lost on me. Even when they didn't make sense.

I have cried more tears and faced more fears than I can count. The biggest fear through all of it was the impact on my family, particularly my kids. As a single mom for most of their lives, I worked extra hard to keep them safe and protect them from the feelings of insecurity I felt as a child. And now, here I was going out on a whim to create something. I wasn't even sure what that something was, so I had no idea what it would require or what was ahead. One of the beauties of settling for fine is that it's safe, familiar and predictable. Now, here I was embarking on something completely unpredictable. Then one day, in the midst of all the uncertainty, my oldest child said to me, "Mom, I'm glad to be watching you learn all of this and do all of this, because I'm learning along with you. That means I won't have to learn it when I'm your age." I've held onto that moment, and others like it from both of my kids. I use those moments of encouragement to remind me why it's no longer okay to settle for "fine." And why it's no longer necessary to live in struggle and endurance. Those moments, those children, my babies are why I need to continue to overcome the stories and limiting beliefs. It's why I need to create something extraordinary – so they can see how. Because even though they have also faced their fair share of struggle and trauma, I refuse to let them settle for anything less than extraordinary.

This journey has been challenging, and it's not one I ever expected to be on. But, wow has it been incredible! I've learned so much about myself and what I'm capable of. I will always consider myself to be strong and resilient (I believe my oldest child has used the word "badass" on more than one occasion and I'm absolutely okay with that). But now, it's time to start mastering the art of dreaming big and creating my own definition of something extraordinary. It's time to nurture a relationship with myself, and to trust that everything I need is within me. It's time to surrender in faith to the idea that I am loved and supported in cultivating a simple, effortless life full of joy, abundance, and love. It's time to overcome!

KARSTA HURD

Karsta Hurd has been a K-12 educator for over 20 years. She is also an international speaker, author and mental fitness coach. She's passionate about personal development and helping others break free from expectations and limiting beliefs. Her nurturing spirit and resilient nature are felt by everyone around her; especially her two beautiful children. You can always find her recharging her emotional battery while sitting by the lake or journaling in her "zen den," always with a cup of coffee in hand. She is most known for empowering others to create their own definition of an extraordinary life with her saying, "Fine Isn't Good Enough."

You can learn more or connect with Karsta at www.karstamarie.com.

Chapter 15

BIRTH OF THE RED BIRD

by Kelly Colley

The sweet calling of the cardinal, the red bird, is one of the sweetest sounds that rings between the rustling of the trees. I often sit on the front porch in the late afternoons as the sun is beginning to set with my eyes closed hearing the sweet song of the wind chimes and just waiting for the song of the red bird. Peacefully, waiting, while watching all the other birds swift by eager to land on the feeder. Grazing for an afternoon snack then whisking away to another branch. Lovely to watch them in flight, as the wind carries under their wings swooping them far up into clouds beyond visible sight. And that quick, they are gone.

I can so perfectly remember the day I found out I was pregnant with you. Sixteen… I knew in the depths of my soul you were mine and nothing would ever take you away from me. Fast forward twenty-four years. I thought you were flourishing, trying to make it on your own in Birmingham. There were text messages, phone calls, and visits that were never long enough to our home. We had long discussions of you moving to the area, getting your real estate license. "I want to make you proud, mama," he would say. I was always so proud. Always so proud of him and his three other brothers.

June 11, 2021, would begin a series of events that would drastically change my outlook on people, my life, and my whole world, even God. I had just come back from a whirlwind vacation from Aruba with some of our bestest friends. I came into work, a corporate position I worked my whole career for to only be released for "lack of communication." I was completely devastated because I knew in my soul that I had worked so extremely hard to get to that point. It was such a gasping moment. The audacity of leadership stating to those around me that I just decided to step down. Lack of communication, God, there has to be a reason! I had visions and goals to work even further up that corporate ladder. What no one knew is that every morning I was throwing up from nerves, drastic weight loss. So even though my flesh wanted it, my spirit was at war and God knew that. He was the only one that knew it. That Monday I got up and regrouped, refocused my mind. I knew that this was not what God had in store for me. He was preparing me for something so much greater. Little did I know that "greater" was a life-altering, devastating nightmare as a mother.

June 16, 2021, I woke up and went into our branch office as normal. Robbie and I had to refocus and try to determine what was next in our lives. He continued to operate as normal; we still had the branch office and team members. I just had to try and figure out what I wanted to do with my real estate license and where I wanted to be and if I even wanted to keep my license with this company. Pierce, my middle child, 22, called almost out of his mind. Explaining he couldn't figure out what was wrong with him. Said he felt crazy, couldn't focus, and was almost depressed. We shared a long conversation about how I was so thankful that he reached out. That it was okay to ask for help. Everyone needs help at times. He paused and said, "Mama, let me call you right back. Pablo keeps calling me." The next call I received was a mama's worst nightmare. Something that crosses every mama's mind when they look at their child, no matter the age they are. I answered the call from Pierce only to hear a blood curdling scream, "MAMA!!! DALTON IS DEAD!" "WHAT, NO!!!!! GOD PLEASE PLEASE NO, PIERCE NO!!!" I immediately fell to the ground, on my knees, screaming to Pierce, "Please tell me this isn't true, not Dalton, not Dalton, God no, please." While my face pressed down against the carpet of the office, balled up like a newborn child, I just cried out to God, why?! I began calling, and calling, and calling his phone. But there was no answer. I screamed from my innermost being, purging vomit on the floor. Feeling like I was dying right then. I instantly felt this feeling of anger and rage come over me that I had never felt before. God no.... after everything I've been through, all these years, and you take my first-born son. The door of the office flew open and it was Susan, a friend and co-worker who works in the same building. She immediately scooped me up in tears, screaming at me, "Kelly, talk to me!!" "He's gone, Susan. He's gone. My baby boy is dead."

As I laid there on the floor sobbing, my whole world was changed forever. Part of me died right there on that floor. "I have to call Robbie," I said. Susan got her assistant to call Robbie, who was the dentist, she then went and picked him up. We rushed home to only discover JW, Dalton's youngest brother, had found out. We packed what we could and then began our five-hour journey to Birmingham straight to Dalton's apartment.

I remember on the way up feeling numb. I mean a deep, dark dumbness, emptiness. Anger and wrath was brewing. At that moment, I knew I would never be the same. Over the next few days we began the process of preparation for peeling back the layers of exactly what had happened. I can remember lying in the bed of the hotel room the first night. We had driven straight into the apartment, but I was too distraught to even enter the apartment. I laid there running through the last conversation we shared, searching through text messages, anything to find any ounce of a clue. I had spoken with the police department and the coroner just a few hours earlier. The corner had explained to me that they had found him lying on his bedroom floor in a fetal position. He had just gotten out of the shower, and wasn't even dressed. He had passed away from a Xanax® laced with fentanyl. But it was ruled as fentanyl poisoning, not suicide. And lying in that bed that night all I could think about was my baby died by himself on that bedroom floor. Over the next five days, which were an absolute blur, we had to have him transported from Birmingham to Montgomery where most of the friends and family were located. I had to make decisions on flowers, memorial service, and eulogy. All the things that a mother should never have to make. I can remember thinking, "I just don't want to do all of this." All the while, the only thing I could cling to was my shattered faith in God. Many conversations with Him always ended with why. Please help me to understand. Two days before the memorial service, I had to sit in a hotel room and write the eulogy for him. I can remember placing a period on the piece of paper and crying. I couldn't write a thing. I had so many beautiful memories, and beautiful things to say about Dalton. His smile and laughter could capture a room. He was so highly intelligent, and an avid baseball pitcher. He loved his brothers and being around family. I simply couldn't wrap my mind, heart, and spirit on what to say. I opened my Bible as I sat there and prayed for God to please speak to me. And He did. He laid the story of Job 2:2-4 on my spirit. And as I read the words, they were like a breath of his glory and His light.

On another day the angels came to present themselves before the Lord, and Satan also came with them to present himself before him. And the Lord said to Satan, "Where have you come from?" Satan answered the Lord, "From roaming throughout the earth, going back and forth on it."3 Then the Lord said to Satan, "Have you considered my servant Job? There is no one on earth like him; he is blameless and upright, a man who fears God and shuns evil. And he still maintains his integrity, though you incited me against him to ruin him without any reason."4 "Skin for skin!" Satan replied. "A man will give all he has for his own life.5 But now stretch out your hand and strike his flesh and bones, and he will surely curse you to your face."6 The Lord said to Satan, "Very well, then, he is in your hands; but you must spare his life."

You see, the first time I walked into Dalton's apartment days before, I prayed before entering. I asked God to please be with me and help me to see him through this darkness. I entered the apartment and immediately I could feel and see that Satan had been roaming around in the space. All the blinds were shut, half the lights wouldn't work, stuff strewn everywhere. It wasn't my Dalton. I could see the depression and could feel the darkness in the room. It pierced my soul and deeply saddened me to know that my baby boy was being attacked. As the tears streamed down my face, I walked into his room and I instinctively knew exactly where he passed away. I laid down on the floor and just cried an uncontrollable gut-wrenching cry. I prayed for God to help me, heal me. Just help me breathe.

Over the last year, I've recreated every situation and circumstance, every flash of traumatized memory in my mind. Searching for Dalton, searching for God, searching for myself. I lost every ounce of who I once was. People who say, "you're so strong," have my heart in their best interest. But when you are faced with this amount of trauma, you have no choice. Absolutely no choice. There were so many days I would lay in bed or on the floor begging God to allow me not to wake up because if I woke up then I would be faced with the reality of him not being here. Even though my faith in God was so strong, I felt betrayed, cheated. I was so angry at God. Yet I never stopped trusting and believing in Him.

I once had a friend tell me it was okay to be mad at God. Our God is big enough to handle all your emotions, because He made them. And that is so true. I have begged God to speak to me and help me understand. And one day He finally did. It was so profound, "Kelly, He was never yours in the first place." I didn't like it and I probably never will, but it was then that I understood. God called him home on June 16, 2021. And as I began to look around, my eyes were opened, really opened. God had shaved a fogged lens off my eyes. I could finally see people, life, and this world as it was always meant to be seen. That scripture from Job was not necessarily meant for me to understand that Dalton was called; it was for me. It was for me to understand that God saved Dalton in that passing moment of him being attacked. Satan knew He couldn't get to me because of my faith so He went after my first-born son. And I know now that Satan thought I would turn against God. But yet, I haven't.

There's so many Godwinks and so many times Dalton has shown up to let me know he's ok. He's truly ok. There's no safer place than at the feet of Jesus Christ. I still don't understand why. But I rest my spirit on John 13:7, *Jesus replied, "You don't understand what I am doing now, but someday you will."* It's not meant for me to understand right now, not in this moment of time. What is meant is for me is to live for God, my children, my husband, my family, and my friends. I am not completely healed and I don't think I ever will be until I rest at His feet. Tomorrow doesn't exist for me anymore. I focus on today, this moment, this second. And that's all I can do. Because it is not promised.

The birth of my red bird, the cardinal. Every day since the passing of Dalton, he comes to visit. The most beautiful, fiery red feathers and the sound of an angel singing. He sings for me every day. Lovely to watch him in flight, as the wind carries under his wings swooping him far up into clouds beyond visible sight. Back to Heaven he returns.

I thank God every time I remember you. And I always pray for all of you with joy. I thank God for the help you gave me while I told people the Good News. You helped from the first day you believed until now. I am sure that the good work God began in you will continue until he completes it on the day when Jesus Christ comes again. I know I am right to think like this about all of you because you are so close to my heart. This is because you have all played such an important part in God's grace to me now during this time that I am in prison, and whenever I am defending and proving the truth of the Good News. God knows that I want very much to see you. I love all of you with the love of Christ Jesus. This is my prayer for you: that your love will grow more and more; that you will have knowledge and understanding with your love; that you will see the difference between what is important and what is not and choose what is important; that you will be pure and blameless for the coming of Christ; that your life will be full of the many good works that are produced by Jesus Christ to bring glory and praise to God.

Philippians 1:3-11

KELLY COLLEY

Kelly Colley currently resides in Orange Beach, Alabama, and loves to write about true life experiences and ways to overcome those experiences through God's grace and understanding his timing. She thoroughly enjoys deep sea fishing, reading, and studying meditation techniques, and enjoys gourmet food. She is happily married to Robb Colley, and they have four boys together, Trey, Dalton, Pierce, and John Walker. They also have three fur babies, Lucy, Frankie, and Cookie. At any day and time, you will more than likely find her close to the water.

Connect with Kelly at

https://www.facebook.com/kellycolleyauthor.

Chapter 16

I AM GOOD ENOUGH

by Kerri Kruger

All my life I have struggled with knowing that I am good enough. All through school I was bullied, but back then it wasn't talked about. It was nothing like it is today. There wasn't social media, cell phones, phones with cameras, or the internet. It was just words said by people that I now know were not happy with themselves. Sadly, though, I let it affect me. Because of the things said by others, it has caused me to doubt my abilities my entire life.

Looking back, I made choices that, had I had the confidence I do now, I would not have made. I turned to food, drinking, and other destructive behaviors, that I understand now were all coping mechanisms that ultimately did not work. They distracted me for a bit from the root cause of my feelings but, in the end, they only enhanced the feelings of worthlessness. They did not help me, but only caused me to question my worth more.

I never felt like I deserved anything that I had, in life and with work. I got jobs I wanted because I knew people, and while I was successful in all that I did, I never felt like I was good enough to be in those positions. I never saw myself as others saw me.

In the spring of 2003, a friend of my parents wanted to fix me up with her son. I had recently gotten out of a relationship that left me feeling worthless. But I agreed to the fix up because it was for a friend. He was a gentleman from the first date and still is today 19 years later. We hit it off and it is one of the best decisions I have ever made. Saying yes to being "fixed up."

Shortly after we started dating, he injured his back and needed lots of assistance daily. He always tells people that God sent me to him since we had only been dating three months when the injury happened. He even gave me the option to bail on the relationship because he knew the long road ahead. I stuck it out, though. I knew there was something there and I wasn't going to let it go that easily.

If I am being honest, though, God sent him to me, too. I was on that destructive path when we met. I was working as a 9-1-1 Operator/Dispatcher on second shift. After work most nights a group of us would go out drinking. Most nights we would close a one o'clock bar and then go to a three o'clock bar and close them down. Other nights we would do that and then someone would go and buy packaged liquor and we would end up back at someone's house and continue drinking into the early hours of the morning. The next day we would turn around and do it all over again. I am not sure how I survived some of what I did.

God knew we needed each other. I needed someone to save me from ruining my life with alcohol, and Jeff was going to need someone to assist and support him after injuring his back. I really feel like Jeff was a gift from God, and he saved me from myself.

To talk about my faith, I feel like we need to go back to the beginning. I was raised going to church every Sunday. Honestly, I went because my parents woke me up every Sunday to go. Don't get me wrong, I believed in God, and enjoyed church and youth group but, again, questioned my self-worth around those people. They were supposed to be Christians, raised by the word of God, but they did and said some of the same hurtful things that the bullies at school did. When we went on trips as the youth group, I would bring a friend along with me to have someone to hang out with and was not reliant on the other members of the group. All these years later, that friend credits me inviting her on those trips to her being a part of that religion today.

After high school, I joined the Army National Guard. While at basic training, I attended church service every Sunday. It was more just a reason to get out of the barracks and away from the drill sergeants for an hour or so; not because my faith was that strong. I made some friends in basic, but nothing long lasting. I didn't keep in touch with any of them afterwards. Again, I didn't feel I was deserving of the friendships I made, and that I wasn't worthy to be someone else's friend.

After I returned from basic training, I moved out and got an apartment with my best friend. We both will admit that it was one of the biggest mistakes we both made. It destroyed our friendship. We didn't agree on things, and we were in different places and, in the end, it just didn't work out. We parted ways and didn't speak for a very long time.

During this time of living on my own, I stopped going to church and began on my path of self-destructive behavior. I joined the local volunteer fire department and got my EMT license. It was shortly after this that I got my job as a dispatcher. I turned 21 and started drinking on a somewhat regular basis.

I later moved to second shift where my drinking really increased and I started jumping from relationship to relationship, thinking I was in love each time. In reality, none of them were love and none of them valued me as a person. They were just an outlet for me, a very negative outlet, that meant nothing, and I regret most all of them. Not to say they all didn't matter, because at the time I felt like they did. But looking back now, most were not relationships, but used as a drug to make me feel like I was wanted by someone, when in most cases it furthered the damage of my thoughts of not being good enough.

I saw a TikTok® recently where this guy talks about believing that you have three loves in your lifetime. There is your first love which happens at a young age, but ultimately ends over nothing. For me this one happened my senior year in high school. He was a few years older, and had baggage, but cared about me. We met while working at a fast-food restaurant and were still together when I was to leave for basic training. I didn't end up going to basic the first time I was scheduled to go because I was overweight by their standards, but when I got back home, I didn't call him right away. In fact, he came over to drop something off to my parents and I hid in my room because I didn't want to see him. The relationship had run its course and I was done. I can't remember exactly why, but I just didn't want the relationship anymore and it ended.

Your second love is a hard one and the one that hurts you. The hurt is caused by lies, betrayal, abuse, and is damaging. But this one teaches us what we love about love and what we don't love about love. It teaches us who the good people are and who the bad people are. As a result, we become closed, careful, cautious, and considerate. This one for me happened while I was working dispatch and is not a relationship that I am proud of for many reasons, but mainly because of how it started. Regardless, I loved this person even though he lied to me, betrayed me, and hurt me. Just as the man describes, after that relationship I became closed off to the thought of dating. I just worried about my work and started back up the destructive behavior of drinking and eating.

Then there is the third love. He says this one will creep up on you silently and happens when you least expect it. You don't go looking for this love, it comes to you. No matter what walls have been built up, they will be broken down. You will find yourself caring about this person without even trying. It is not the usual person you would find yourself going after, but you want marriage and a family with them. You truly love them.

It had only been eight months since the second love of my life. I had sworn off dating for a while, especially if they had previously been married, and/or had children. I remember it clearly. I was at lunch with my best friend, the one that I had gotten an apartment with. We reconciled after some time and are still close today. My mom called me about the family friend who was wanting to set me up with their son. He was divorced and had a 7-year-old daughter. I immediately told my mom I was not interested. I did not want anything to do with someone with that kind of past. But my mom convinced me to talk to him and maybe it would be good to have him as a friend.

As I previously mentioned, we hit it off and 19 years later we are still together. The relationship was rough in the beginning. I was still struggling with not feeling good enough and continuing with my drinking, which caused many arguments. But as I mentioned in the beginning, I stood by him, and he stood by me, for reasons I am still not sure about today, but I am forever thankful that he did.

He broke down those walls that I had built up and finally made me feel loved in the way I deserved to be loved. I still had my struggles. There was still something missing. After everything we went through with his injury, a friend reached out to him and invited us to attend his church. Neither of us had attended church in years and took him up on the offer. It was a very small church and we loved it. Jeff started playing guitar for the praise team and he also played in a Christian band with the friend that had invited us, the pastor and the praise team leader. We had great times.

One night the church did a viewing of the *Passion of the Christ*. As a baby, my parents had me baptized, so I never made that decision for myself, which is what their faith believed. The church we were attending was Baptist, and after seeing that movie, I felt strongly moved to be baptized by emersion. I shared this decision with the pastor and made the commitment that night to be baptized. We did that at a Sunday service, and I am convinced God has a sense of humor since the hot water heater went out that morning, so I was submerged in ice cold water for my baptism. But I did it! I had committed my life back to God and have not turned back since.

It has been a long road for me and something I still struggle with daily, but finally, with my belief in God, I know that I am good enough. My life is not defined by what bullies say to me or about me. I am not defined by what anyone thinks about me. There are still times that those thoughts creep in, but I know that is the devil's work and he is trying to destroy me and pull me away from my belief in God. My faith is strong and I have surrounded myself with likeminded people who build me up, not break me down, and help me believe daily that I AM GOOD ENOUGH!

KERRI KRUGER

Kerri Kruger is a wife, mother, daughter, and friend. She has a heart of gold and will do anything for not only her family and friends, but anyone in need. Always looking for ways to get involved in the community, she is constantly on the go. But she is an overcomer, battling her own thoughts of her own self-worth. She has learned she is good enough!

Connect with Kerri on Facebook at

https://www.facebook.com/kerri.pattersonkruger/.

Chapter 17

INSIDE MY ADHD BRAIN: CYCLING FROM TOXIC OVERWHELM TO CREATIVE SYNERGY

by Dr. Leigh Holcomb, PhD, ELI-MP

I can't think! My brain has switched into the OFF position. If my head wasn't stuck onto my shoulders, I would lose it along with my keys, my phone, various papers that I was supposed to sign for my child's school, and all of the left socks that go through the laundry. What is wrong with me?

Have thoughts similar to these ever gone through your mind? Some days, your mind is clear and bright and you are highly productive at work and home. Then, BAM, now you are stuck in the "Land of I Don't Know." In a world that is geared to value consistency, it is soooo easy to feel like a total failure. Your emotions go swirling to the conclusion that you just aren't that smart. "I'm not good enough," is your mantra as you try to measure up to a standard that might as well be the Olympic high jump.

I first felt truly overwhelmed in the third grade as the 9 times multiplication table became the daily homework demon that I needed to fight. I would jump from foot to foot as if I could jiggle the answer out of my brain and then end up in tears. Despite hours of drilling by my dad with multiplication flashcards, I just couldn't pull out the answer to the question of "what is 9x7?" from my memory.

I found out that I LOVED science in fourth grade when the very first scientist that I had ever met came to my elementary school to teach marine biology. Marianne Coultier's enthusiasm was infectious and I still remember a beach field trip to collect specimens like hermit crabs and baby fish from among submerged mangrove roots. My lifelong fascination with the brain began not long after. How could this 3-pound piece of biological material be responsible for walking, talking, and thinking profound thoughts about God? The teachers that I encountered in 4th grade convinced me that I was bright and capable of becoming a scientist.

My optimism was crushed by my 6th grade math teacher, Mr. L, who seemed determined to prove that I was stupid. More tears over math occurred when he called me up to the chalkboard to work a problem in front of class. This activity was the bane of my existence and the cause of much stress. I still remember the smell of the chalk dust and the sound of the chalk softly screeching across the blackboard as the other students seemed to write the answer as if by magic while I stood frozen with the chalk in my hand staring at the math problem. "You'll never learn to do math" was what I recall Mr. L to have said as he told me to put down the chalk and go back to my seat. Someone snickered with suppressed laughter as I walked down the aisle to my seat and sat down with my head hung low and tears in my eyes. I brought home my first D on a report card with a sense of shame. I remember feeling so very stupid and worthless as I showed the report card to my mom.

What happened next never ceases to amaze me. My mom made an appointment to talk to my math teacher and her words still ring in my memory. "My daughter is NOT a D student. If she isn't getting the math information, then it has to do with the way that you are teaching it." In my eyes, my mom was like an Avenging Angel sent from God with a flaming sword of truth that cut through the negativity and fear that Mr. L spread to his students in his 6th grade math classroom. "Well, I don't think it will help but there is a box of materials in the back of the classroom that she can try" was his response. Without the shame-based teaching shutting down my brain, I quickly pulled my math grade up.

The rest of my high school and college career showed a similar pattern of periods of great focus and achievement followed by running into stumbling blocks due to inattention. My love of science was a point of laser focus. As I was close to completing a Bachelor's degree in Biology from New College, I had the first real career conversation of my life when my Dad asked, "What are you going to do with your biology degree?" I had been so focused on completing the degree that I had forgotten that at some point I would need to get a job and support myself. My reply was a very profound, "I don't know. I guess I will go to graduate school." So, I did for a very long time!

A neuroscience program flyer from the University of Southern California posted on the biology department bulletin board was a life-changer. USC had not even been on my radar as I was on the east coast, but I decided to put in my application to USC along with several other neuroscience graduate programs. I prayed that God would open one door so that I would clearly know what school I should attend. The long wait in faith began.

One rejection letter after another came in the mail saying, "Thank you for your application, but we regret to inform you that you have not been selected to join our program." A battle with discouragement started as with each letter came the realization that my math skills might not be good enough to allow me to pursue the career path that I had chosen. What I learned was that if you pray that God will open only one door, you should expect that all the others will be firmly bolted shut to keep you from wandering through them. A shout of joy went up to heaven when I finally saw the words, "You have been accepted into the University of Southern California Neuroscience Program."

While I was overjoyed that I had gotten accepted, the reality that I was moving across the United States from Florida to California to live in Los Angeles was hard to wrap my head around. My career path changed abruptly when the city of Los Angeles erupted into flames in

1992 during the Rodney King riots. A friend and I drove out of the city to safety as the National Guard was driving into Los Angeles. When I returned, the convenience store around the corner from my apartment had been burned down. I wrestled with the decision of should I stay or should I leave?

A conversation with a pair of USC professors showed me the open door as they were leaving Los Angeles to move to Tampa to open an Alzheimer's Research lab at the University of South Florida. I left Los Angeles with a job in hand as their lab manager. The prayer of "Lead me on your path, God" had taken me off the career path that I had mapped out and the move brought me back full circle to my hometown and my family. In this phase of my life, I learned to be proactively prepared to go through life's needed transitions in a resilient manner.

However, I was still primarily living on borrowed faith asking others like my mom and grandmother to pray for me, but having little conversation with God on my own. I finished a Ph.D. at the University of South Florida, married and moved to Texas to begin a post-doc at Texas A&M. I was firmly on the academic career path to success when I was promoted to Assistant Professor.

God has a plan to reach those who wander far from their faith. During a trip to New Orleans, I was handed a slip of paper by a street preacher as I passed by. I went into my hotel room intending to throw away the piece of paper. As I looked at this small slip of paper, I saw the face of Jesus wearing the crown of thorns on his head and the Holy Spirit moved in my heart. I began to cry and rededicated myself to follow God that night. That "chance encounter" with a complete stranger was a turning point in my life.

While my career and faith were flourishing, my marriage was crumbling. When my baby girl was just six months old, I became a single mom through divorce. Juggling solo parenting while being the family breadwinner was a stress that was relieved by joining a single mom's bible study at my church. There I found friends who were thrilled to hold my baby, share parenting advice, and sit with me in church as they encouraged me to grow in my faith.

God draws close to the broken hearted. One night, I laid face down on the cold tile bathroom floor, listening for the baby to cry and praying to God that she would remain asleep. My body had been overwhelmed by the stomach virus that my child had brought home from daycare. As a divorced parent, I had been up repeatedly for the prior two weeks washing sheets and tending to a baby who was miserable from projectile vomiting with no one in the house to provide a respite. An angel in the form of another mom saw me standing bewildered in the grocery store in front of the array of different formulas and told me about a formula that would be very gentle on my baby's stomach. That encounter solidified my decision to always be generous in passing along information to others that might lift their burdens.

Trusting in the Lord was the lesson of the following phase of my life. My next career transition came in the form of a message from Human Resources. "I'm sorry, Dr. Holcomb, we aren't going to be able to renew your contract. Due to budget restrictions, there was a unilateral decision to lay off people with new contracts in two weeks." I just signed a three-year contract a month earlier. The message came on my birthday and the day before I was scheduled to host an Alzheimer's conference.

"Blessed are those who trust in the LORD and have made the LORD their hope and confidence" (Jeremiah 17:7 NLT) became my scripture focus as I learned to wait on the Lord. On the last hour of the last day before I needed to turn in my keys, an extension to my contract came through. A seemingly "random" meeting with a sales representative soon after led me to a 10-year career in the pharmaceutical industry.

I had an aha moment at a conference on ADHD in Women & Girls when I heard Dr. Patricia Quinn say, "All women with ADHD are desperate housewives." Many of my struggles to keep things organized and tendency to wait, due to difficulty keeping track of time, could be due to the inattentive subtype of ADHD. I wasn't stupid, lazy, or morally slack. My brain just works differently. I had to unlearn long-held habits of thinking in order to create a life and workplace that was kind to my brain rather than burning it out. Once my daughter got into school, I realized that she also had a brain that works differently (ADHD, dyslexia, and a math learning disability called Dyscalculia). I was over 50 when I finally realized that I most likely had Dyscalculia as well as ADHD. A book called *Grace Based Parenting* by Tim Keller was key in helping me to realize that I was blessed to help this bright, loving child grow into all her energetic, creative potential.

As the CEO of Career Catalyst Edge, I'm passionate about helping women working in the pharma and biotech industries to integrate their God-given strengths and create career paths that align with their values.

DR. LEIGH HOLCOMB

Dr. Leigh Holcomb, ELI-MP is the CEO of Career Catalyst Edge, a life science career coaching company.

With over a decade of experience in the pharmaceutical industry as a Medical Science Liaison and Executive Recruiter, she uses her academic and industry experience to support mid-career professionals in pharma and biotech as they transition successfully to their next job opportunity or promotion. Having been on both sides of the interview table, Leigh has a unique perspective and is passionate about helping others find their dream job and career path. She is a speaker at Life Science conferences and an advocate for the advancement of Women in Science.

Trained as a Neuroscientist, raising awareness of ADHD in girls and women as well an underrecognized math learning disability called Dyscalculia are part of Leigh's current educational efforts. In 2022, she joined the Board of Directors for RIZE Prevention, which focuses on school-age drug prevention and intervention. In the past, she has helped to establish a faith-based ministry to provide respite care for individuals with Alzheimer's disease and led a ministry for single moms.

Leigh is based near Greenville, South Carolina, where she shares a multi-generational household with her joy-filled mom and her creative daughter who is a future animator. If she could tell you one thing, it would be, "Take care of your brain because it's the only one you've got!"

Connect with Dr. Holcomb at www.careercatalystedge.com.

Chapter 18

SHE HAS OVERCOME...

by Linsey A Jorgenson

The ability to overcome. To fight fear and fight through the pains in life. It starts with the knowledge that our perfect Lord and Savior has the absolute best plan for all of us and He ALWAYS shows up. I repeat to those of you reading this – HE WILL SHOW UP FOR YOU. HE WILL FIGHT FOR YOU. The key is faith. Trusting Him to handle our battles and amen! Because if you are like me...life's challenges can be overwhelming.

I had my life planned out. I had all the "things" that checked the box of success – and an impressive shoe collection, I might add! However, I was becoming more and more restless with this so-called success. I couldn't stop reflecting on the meaning of life and asking God "why did you create me?" I was unfulfilled and underwhelmed at the mundane "rat race" of the corporate world. More importantly, I kept reflecting on the thought of "when I die...what will I say that I have done?" What kingdom impact am I making now? If it's God's will that I follow what the world defines as success...then why am I miserable? I just couldn't accept that what I (keyword "I") was doing was really His plan for my life.

So...I did something I NEVER thought I would do. I overcame my fear and stepped out in faith. I went on a mission trip to Haiti. I hate flying (fear!) and going to the poorest country in the Western Hemisphere was unnerving and scary (fear!). I stayed up all night before the early flight praying for safety and trying to ignore my pounding heart and upset stomach and the ugly "what if's" that kept running through my head. Little did I know that this trip would forever change the trajectory of my life and ruin all those "perfect plans" I had made. (And yet, still somewhat continue to do. Why? Because it makes me feel more comfortable to think I have it figured out, and time and again – He changes my plans. Thank you, God! These plans I make are a security blanket for me and he continues to patiently teach me that He is my security.)

My "one year" plan (only ONE year!) to serve the impoverished in Haiti has turned into 11 years!

My first year was challenging. I couldn't speak the local language and, as a foreigner in a dangerous country, that's scary (fear!). I was volunteering for another organization at the time, and I was out of my element. I never experienced the amount of poverty I saw in Haiti.

However, I chose to overcome that fear by stepping into a committed relationship with the Lord and trusting Him to protect, lead, and guide me. To help relieve stress, I would jog through town at the end of the long, hot days. It helped alleviate the pain and poverty I saw daily, which caused stress and sorrow on my tender heart.

That's when I met a group of kids that were living on the street. When I went to a restaurant, I would see these same kids sleeping by the entrance – and I would have to step over them. Then, I felt obligated to buy food for them. I learned quickly how dangerous that is.

Rather quickly, we formed a bond. They were outcasts and I was an outsider. I didn't feel I had a place. These kids didn't have a place. So, they started running alongside me – barefoot. I was becoming increasingly aware that street children "disappear" so starting a running program was my way of keeping track of them and gave them a purpose. We all had found a place...together.

Rather than give them hand-outs (which perpetuates the shame of the impoverished), I decided to spend time with them. I learned about their life, started visiting the ghettos where they find community, and stepped into my fear to accept those that are not what I know. I began to live a life not desired, but a life to honor those that deserved change.

This then led me to a different kind of overcoming. Overcoming the discouragers, the negativity and, in general, the faith-less. It came from all directions. The locals told me street kids were worthless and not to be trusted. "Don't waste your time," they told me. Those in the US were fearful for my safety. "It's too risky and too challenging," they told me. Even worse were the lies I kept hearing in my own head, disguised as truths. "You aren't smart enough to do this. You can't start a nonprofit. WHO ARE YOU to think you could do something like that?" However, in those quiet times there was a resounding… "my child, not you but Me…and you can do this. Because it is me, in you. Are you willing to answer My calling? You did ask Me, remember?" And so, I overcame the doubts and fear and said, "Ok, I trust You."

Not everyone is called to another country, but we are all called to overcome our fear, because fear is a lie from the one that does not want us to do anything for His kingdom. How many times have we visited our local Starbucks® or a Chick-fil-A® or Walmart® and noticed that maybe someone is silently suffering. You get that feeling and a still small voice says "do something kind" and then quickly we decide no, that's weird. It's weird to talk to a stranger. It's uncomfortable. No, we need to move on about the day with errands and all the busy-ness we have in our lives.

I had to stop being about "me" and start really listening to that still small voice. And, the small voices surrounding me…the kids that were begging me for a safe place to sleep and the ability to take a shower with soap and brush their teeth. Little eyes wide and wet, looking at me with the question "will you please help us?"

So…against all odds, I created a homeless shelter for the youth in Haiti. It happened so fast that I couldn't believe it. As God does. There were a few people that believed in the vision God gave me. The resounding comment I kept stating to everyone I knew…"we have to

TRY." I felt I owed it to these kids to try and if it doesn't work…well then, we at least stepped out in faith and took the chance. It was time to find a makeshift home and get those doors open before something terrible happened to these kids that deserved to know why they were created and who their Father was. I knew it would take time to find a shelter…but, in the meantime, we did what we could. We started "street church" and the slogan was "no shoes no problem." We started doing basic medical care and pouring into the kids about who they were. For the kids that didn't know their names – we gave them one. For the many that had no idea how old they were…we gave them ages and birthdays and celebrated that.

And then…I awoke to the smell of burning. I thought, ok – someone was burning food in the kitchen? Maybe? I touched the doorknob to my bedroom and immediately I knew. My house was on fire. In that moment – shockingly – I was calm. I resigned to the fact that this was it…and in that moment I asked our Lord "is this really how I am going to die?" I decided that if I was going to burn to death anyway – I might as well fight for the chance to survive. I grabbed a towel and opened the door. I fell back from the heat and the cloud of smoke that hit like a wall. The smoke was thick. I saw that I had maybe six inches from the smoke to the floor and then I had to shut my eyes from the burn. I covered my mouth with the towel and crawled to knock on the other two bedroom doors in the house. Get out! Try! And then blind…I crawled all the way to the door and down the stairs. I had no time to think. I got out and began banging on the neighbors' doors. "HELP! FIRE! There is still someone in there!" I sat below in shock that I made it out, which was a miracle, and then watched all my things burning to the ground, convinced our house manager had died already. After the neighbors banned together tossing buckets of water…hours later, he walked out. His room had a fire-proof door. The house went up, and he had no idea. (Where was the fire department you ask? They showed up…and quickly discovered they had no water. Haiti. Props to the neighbors that saved countless homes and ended the fire before it caught the other homes attached!)

Crawling through the flames – already thinking I'm going to burn to death. Then, sitting and watching the house devour the things I loved. Coveted, to be frank. The material things. And just days before the shelter opening. I so badly wanted to run, quit, throw in the towel, and just give up. So, I flew to Florida and my Dad met me there. He encouraged me that no matter what – He supported me. He brought me clothes, toiletries, and just sat and listened to my tears. Yes, listening to tears is a thing. It's when you remain quiet and sit in the pain alongside the one suffering. You just remain…there. Present.

Just like my Dad, our LORD is always present. There. Listening to the tears. In the most difficult situations, discouragement and pain and fear are waiting to devour you. So…you praise the Lord in the most difficult situation and circumstance. You focus on Him. You DIVE into Him. You thank Him! You overcome!

The biggest challenge - how do I overcome my own feelings? You don't accept that your feelings are reality. This is where Satan loves to destroy. You speak into the Word and trust that He will handle it. The bad things in your head running rampant and wreaking havoc are not of the Father that loves you!

From the start – I was told these kids will never change. Those would be the kids that helped rebuild that house. Those would be the kids that accelerated in schools that told them they could never enter.

To date…we have three facilities, caring for almost 200 children, with plans to open two more centers and beyond. Where God calls us – we will go!

My story is one thing – but the countless stories of the kids here is another. The ones that hear "you will never amount to anything," and yet – OVERCOME!

LISTEN TO ME LADIES OF THE ONE TRUE LORD – every possible thing that comes to us, every pain, every heart-stabbing

SHE IS AN OVERCOMER

circumstance– it was ordained because we can handle it and it is NOT of HIM! HE WILL HANDLE IT! (Shout out to Job!)

This book is for ignition, my sisters! Do not dwell in the suffering and do not accept it. Step out in your beautiful self! Do not sit in the suffering, but ignite in the overcoming!

The kids who everyone said were worthless – those were the kids that rebuilt the house.

The people who tell you "you can't" will be the ones you end up helping.

Those who tell you the passion that drives you, inside you, is a waste of time, are the very people you are ordained to help. To pour into.

Is it easy? No chance. However, our calling is not meant to be easy – it's meant to be fruitful and the joy and peace amidst the longsuffering…it's the still small voice.

Thank you for allowing me to share this story. By sharing this with you I overcame again…my fear of writing and sharing (because "who am I?").

I am the daughter of the King of this world who will always do the miraculous within us. And, you are, too.

LINSEY JORGENSON

Linsey Jorgenson was born December 8, 1982, on the side of the highway. She arrived a month early and did NOT want to miss Christmas! (She was head-strong and determined before she even entered the world!)

Linsey grew up in northern Virginia. She is a graduate of East Carolina University (2005) with a bachelor's in Communication. She is a proud Alpha Phi sister! (AOE for life!)

"Will you step out on the water? Will you listen to My voice and serve whole-heartedly and sacrificially? You serve comfortably - will you get uncomfortable for Me?"

Linsey has lived in Cap-Haitien, Haiti, for the past 11 years. She founded Streethearts Haiti, a nonprofit organization that helps street children. To date, Streethearts has three locations, serving almost 200 children and counting...

Linsey's walk with the Lord has grown exponentially, although not evenly. She has had her share of tumbles. She stands firm in actively pursuing her purpose and the twists and turns that come along with abandoning her plans in order to follow His plan for her and His organization that she serves.

God doesn't need us to accomplish His plan. He invites us to join Him, wherever that is and whatever that means. She rests in that and Him.

Linsey hopes her story inspires others to listen to that inner voice, to step up and out – right where you are – your home, your community, or anywhere in this great big world that God calls you to be!

Connect with Linsey at www.streetheartshaiti.org.

Chapter 19

AM I EVER GOING TO BE OKAY? LIKE, REALLY OKAY?

by Madi Riley

Am I ever going to be okay? Like, really okay? I've asked myself this question a million times before and the short answer is that... maybe, because it all works out one day. Right?

At a very young age, I learned how to be strong, how to cloak my fear with bravery, how to smile with a broken heart, laugh when I was in the most pain, and stay calm when it felt like the world was caving in. I knew how to become the perfect patient, and when I let my guard down, I knew how to put it back up. I knew just how much strength I needed to show in order to get myself and everyone around me through the worst years. Honestly, I was amazed at how easy this was. I was stuck in a body and mind where entropy reigned supreme, but all I had to do was smile and nod and the world would recognize me as the kid who was calm despite everything she was going through. "It's okay," I told myself, "If I keep my fear hidden, I can keep everyone else safe. If I am doing good, then there is one less thing for them to worry about."

In 2009 I was diagnosed with Nephrotic Syndrome and Focal Segmental Glomerulosclerosis (FSGS). FSGS is a chronic kidney disease that causes scarring on your kidneys' filters, which renders the kidneys unable to filter a person's blood properly, ultimately leading to kidney damage and failure. I was seven years old at the time and obsessed with Hannah Montana®, Barbie® dolls, M&M's®, and the color yellow. I have very little memory of the time before my diagnosis, or the first six years after. In fact, the memories I do have are as intelligible as if you were reading a book with sections of pages missing throughout. There is really no way for my mind to paint a clear picture of what I went through. Most of what I do remember consists of Rainbow Loom® bracelets, One Direction on full volume in my earbuds, and lots of orange Jell-O®. I have clung to stories told by my family about those first six years spent in a constant cycle in-and-out of a hospital and declared them to be my experience. It's nightmarish not remembering what happened or how I felt and dealt with it all. To have my only memories of those first six years after diagnosis be the experiences of those around me, I have a hard time accepting it as "my story" to tell, even though it really is *my story* to tell. Regardless of how blurry and enigmatic those years were for me, they still happened to me. I'll spare you the details of those first six years, which consisted mostly of check-ups with my nephrologist and labs. The important thing is that while the future of my health was consistently unknown, my condition was stable. The main concern was getting the elementary aged child to learn how to swallow pills properly. After that, things were solid… until they weren't.

In January of 2014, my nephrologist informed us that my FSGS was causing my kidney function to worsen. We were told that within the next five years, I would need a kidney transplant. Two weeks later, I got the flu. I was hospitalized and we learned that the virus had seriously affected my kidney function, making the worsened function even worse. It was a seven-day hospital stay, during which I became severely ill. When I did start to feel better, I went home where I rested for a week before returning to the hospital for 18 more days. A greater extent of medical interference was now needed in order to keep me stable. I was confused. What was happening to my body? How could I be this sick when I felt fine? Even though I didn't understand, I put on my brave face and pretended to make sense of it all. I had a PowerPICC®

line placed in my chest in order for me to receive albumin infusions at home, which helped control my disease. With this, I remained fairly healthy for the rest of 2014, and I savored every minute I had outside of the hospital. Even with that PowerPICC® line stuck in my chest, and the doubt running circles in my mind, I was grateful to be "healthy." I knew the direction we were headed and took in every good moment, however, still very much anticipating the day my world would be turned upside down. That day came in January of 2015 after my second kidney biopsy. The results determined that my FSGS was progressing quickly. In just one year, I went from having a 75% kidney function to a 25% kidney function. With such a fast rate of progression, dialysis and kidney transplantation were going to be needed within the year for me to survive. From there, everything happened really fast. A peritoneal dialysis catheter was placed in my stomach and I had my first treatment in March. My family, friends, and community rallied around me in support. They held prayer circles, fundraisers, benefits, and sent an overwhelming amount of love my way. I felt lifted by immense prayer and devotion, without which I would not have made it through.

I was on dialysis for nine months. I was hooked up to a large machine for ten hours every night. I would wake up every morning, after a full-night's sleep, only to feel completely drained. I would be lying if I told you I didn't lose hope somewhere along the way. I was insecure, depressed, anxious, and afraid of what was going to happen next. I lack a lot of clarity of what all happened within those nine months. My treatment fogged my brain and took away the energy I needed to be present with my experience. But I vividly remember this thought that I had one Wednesday night when I woke up to use the bathroom, "What would happen if I just don't re-start the machine when I lay back down? Will that be the end? Will it kill me? I think that would be okay." At fourteen years old, that was a scary thought to have, and I had no idea what it meant. I just knew that I hated how I was living. "Living." I laugh at that word when I think about my life then. The treatment I received through my PowerPICC® line and dialysis both kept me alive, but to say that I was *living* would be a joke because life on machines doesn't exist. There were so many days where I questioned, "why?" and felt completely hopeless and lost. I was not convinced I would ever be okay again. My Hannah Montana® loving, Rainbow Loom® making, One Direction listening, orange Jell-O® eating childhood spark was gone.

Later on that same year, I got a letter in the mail that read, "This letter is to confirm that Madison has been placed on the kidney waiting list with the United Network for Organ Sharing (UNOS) on August 26, 2015." During my time on the waitlist, my parents and other family members went through a series of tests to determine if they would be a match for donation. I was blessed with several matches within my family, and it was my dad who donated his kidney. Our surgery took place on December 7th, 2015. My surgery lasted five hours and I remember waking up feeling very at peace with the pain. Like, maybe I was going to be okay? I knew there were risks involved. It was possible to lose the new kidney to rejection, which is when your body's immune system treats the new organ like a foreign object and attacks it. I knew there was a chance my FSGS could return to my new kidney. It was always made clear to me that this surgery was just another treatment… not a cure. But my transplant has given me years of life that never would have existed otherwise; six really beautiful years. With each year that passed, my fear of acquiring the risks of a kidney transplant faded. I was going to school, meeting new people, finding new passions, and having fun. I was *living*. Maybe I was going to be okay. Like, really okay.

The day after my 20th birthday I began running a fever of 102. I tested positive for COVID-19 a few days later and was bedridden for two weeks. Being immunocompromised made having COVID-19 scary. With each day I wasn't getting better, I feared for the worst. Luckily, at some point during those blurry days, I started feeling better. I ended up neglecting my monthly labs because of how sick I was and the quick pace of my life afterwards. Not just once, though. I skipped out on three months of numbers that clue us into the condition of my kidney transplant - my source of life for the past six years. Eventually, I had a routine clinic visit and labs with my nephrologist.

I get anxious before every appointment, no matter what it is. White-coat syndrome drags me into the triage room headfirst as fast as it can and completely takes over my body the second I sit down. But this day was different. I was anxious, but it felt more like another Thursday than anything. I was breathing easy and feeling confident. I was ready for the usual medication adjustment, reminder to keep drinking plenty of water, and pat on the back to send me on my way. Aside from skipping my monthly labs, I'd been doing a great job at following all of the rules in the kidney patient playbook. My mom and I were sent back to a check-up room after the nurse checked my vitals. I sat on the big, tissue-covered table and swung my feet while we waited for the doctors to come in. When they did, they were warm, like usual. But within minutes, I went from feeling comfort, to chaos. The news we got that day was the kind of news that slaps you in the face, turns you upside down, and twists knots in your stomach, to the point where you're not sure whether or not you have the ability to stand, speak, or breathe anymore. My labs indicated signs that my FSGS was recurring in my transplanted kidney. The shock came from the fact that after five years of transplantation, the likelihood of recurrence is really low. I was trying not to panic; to remain calm and focus on the positive news. There was a fix for recurrence and, for that, I was thankful. I spent every Friday the next four weeks getting an infusion of a medication called Rituximab®. The doctors noted that if all went well with the treatment, I would be in remission by the start of 2022. The infusions were easy and I didn't drown in negative side-effects. I experienced a lot of fatigue, but that was normal. The fourth and final infusion was administered on New Year's Eve. I stayed up until midnight to make a toast to a happy and healthy New Year.

The doctors gave my body time to take in the effects of the infusions before re-checking my labs. The results showed that my numbers were stable, but I was not in remission. One thing is for certain… I tend to feel pretty weak and defeated when I lose control over my health. There's only so much I can do: take my meds on time, eat right, drink enough water, check my blood pressure, stay active, etc.… everything else is out of my control and I was having to re-learn how to be okay with that. Another kidney biopsy was performed to get an accurate picture of the new FSGS and a week later we got the results.

"We can confirm that your FSGS has returned, and it returned with a vengeance on your new kidney. We are also seeing very clear chronic rejection in your kidney, which at this stage has caused irreversible damage." When I heard those words, I went numb. I simultaneously had a million thoughts running through my mind and none at all. I just sat there, quietly, next to my mom until the call ended.

I am 21 now and living with a re-diagnosis of FSGS and chronic rejection. I know that I will need dialysis and another transplant to survive. I'm not sure what is to come, and the uncertainty leaves me wondering…

Am I ever going to be okay? Like, really okay? The short answer is that, maybe… because it all works out one day. Right? The long answer is that I went on a walk one day and cried at how beautiful the sunset was. I started my first day of a new job that I love. I celebrated receiving my associates degree with cupcakes and the young woman behind the counter told me to "have a happy day!" And so, I did. I went on more walks and watched more sunsets. I think that life is brutal at times, and there is only so much you can do when you lose control of your own. I think a nice walk and a sunset that brings tears to your eyes are the little things worth celebrating. Am I ever going to be okay? Like, really okay? I think because of all of this, and everything that is to come, the final answer is yes… because it all works out one day. I promise.

MADI RILEY

Madi Riley is a passionate activist, professional empath, and aspiring educator. She becomes easily enraptured with stories - reading them, writing them, vanishing within them.

Madi attends Eastern Illinois University where she is studying Elementary Education and Creative Writing. She resides in the one and only Farmer City, Illinois, with her chaotic and convivial family.

In 2020, Madi began sharing her personal passion for writing with her close friends and family, exploring her journey through health crisis, mental illness, and entering her twenties. Madi shares her writing publicly for the first time in Dara Bose and Lynda Sunshine West's *She Is an Overcomer*.

Connect with Madi at https://www.instagram.com/madihouser/.

Chapter 20

IMAGINE WILDLY: A STORY OF HEALING

by Mary Beth Vieira

I don't know what it is about a bathroom floor that heralds a wake-up call, but it did for me, especially since I was lying there and couldn't get up. The cold tile felt harsh and unforgiving, yet it was there holding me up, an awful refuge as I lay on my side in a semi-fetal position. The dirty corners, lint, and strands of fallen hair stared accusingly at my face, but there was nothing to be done about them. I couldn't clean it, or make anything better, not myself, not my surroundings, not my life. Time stood as still as my body, stuck in the overwhelming horror of it all and a sinking, dreadful feeling that this was my life. This experience, right now. This. Is. My. One. Life. It was supposed to be something beautiful, right? But instead, I was in the full throes of a "reaction" to something, who knows what, but vowing to myself I would never, ever, ever, again eat whatever it was that my body had this time taken particular offense to. Between the vomiting, diarrhea, full body pain and uncontrolled shaking, blood pressure spikes and crashes that left me blacking out over and over, I also heard a sound coming from deep in my throat, probably a combination of crying and a panic attack because my heart was breaking, and my body already had. Although I had struggled with illness off and on due to multiple immune mediated diseases since childhood, this was the moment that I began wondering if this was it. Was this my life? Was I going to continue to get worse? I thought about my children. They were still so young. Would I get to see them grow up?

How long would this misery continue until I eventually faded away forever? I felt cheated out of life. It seemed like it might be over or at least the beginning of the end for me.

Three months prior to this particular incident (yes, there were many!), I had begun doing sessions with a very strange and "woo-woo" type of therapist. She was initially recommended to me by a health coach I had seen once. After completing my assessment, coach Amy rightly decided my health problems were much deeper than diet and lifestyle changes could fix, and she referred me to Robin. Dr. Robin Perry Braun was a psychologist and Christian minister that created a modality called the Integrated Life Process, which combines aspects of body, mind, and spirit health with quantum energy principles. Robin began working with me to reprogram limiting beliefs and heal past trauma, and I followed along with somewhat of a "raised eyebrows" attitude. I was the cynical skeptic, doubting Thomas, a product of the 'show me' state and upbringing in a religious cult which taught me to be afraid and untrusting of everything unfamiliar or outside its very reclusive programming. While I knew I had trauma from my childhood and beyond, I didn't anticipate that addressing it would do anything for my health, but if I could stop the terrifying recurring nightmares I had of being back in the cult and unable to leave, then I thought Robin's method was worth a try. In the sessions I had done with Robin by this point, I learned a little about meditating for a specific purpose to create a shift in energy or raise your vibration.

Which takes me back to the bathroom floor.

As I was lying on that shamefully dirty floor, feeling the depth of hopeless despair and re-cycling thoughts that were various versions of "is this all I get out of life," I had momentary inspiration. What if I thought about something that would help raise my vibration? It sounded nice, like a tall, iced tea, tree shade and cool breeze on a blistering midwest summer day kind of nice. I remembered Robin saying that God created us with an imagination and we use it all the time in a negative way called "worry," but rarely do we think it is good and ok to use our imagination in a positive way. This seemed dangerously close to fantasizing I thought, pointless, unrealistic, and borderline (or totally!) sinful.

Even though it felt entirely impossible, I decided to imagine for a minute. I thought about how I wanted to feel. I wanted to feel strong, healthy, able, ALIVE, happy, peaceful, maybe the way I would feel if I was kayaking on a lake instead of immobile on a disgusting bathroom floor. I had never kayaked on a lake before or anywhere for that matter as my upbringing did not allow individual recreation, but I remember having a desire to kayak even as a young child that must've originated from a beautiful glossy photograph in a magazine such as National Geographic, because we had those.

I imagined as wildly as I could while I laid there, visualizing myself in the distance. The kayak was red and my figure indistinct, but the water…Oh! The water shimmered with a thousand promises, reflecting light back and forth in a hypnotic dance. Green rose gently from each side of the lake, melting into a remote bluish gray haze while the air and sky appeared impossibly clear, a brief fluff of white floated here and there like afterthoughts. Drawn back to the kayak, I saw a flash from each end of the paddle as it rose and fell in a steady, methodical rhythm and felt…peace.

"*That is my story,*" I whispered to myself.

"That is my end," I continued, "not this bathroom floor. This might be something I am experiencing, but it is only a chapter in my story. *This is not where I am going.* **That**… the lake, the kayak, the amazing feeling of peace and happiness and health, ***that is where I am going.*** *That is my story!*"

And I believed myself, for a moment anyway. I felt like I was there, in this space I had intentionally created with my mind and heart. In his book, *The Biology of Belief*, stem cell biologist Bruce Lipton says that our cells are listening to our thoughts and beliefs and behave accordingly. In that moment of connected, intentional thought/belief/feeling, I experienced a subtle energy shift in my body. My breathing calmed and the nausea eased just enough to find the edge of relief. My body responded slowly and I raised myself up onto all fours, crawled into my room and into bed.

The meditation I created that day was one I returned to several times in my healing journey. On the bad days, when the vomiting wouldn't stop, when the pain deep in my bones and the burning on the surface of my skin made me want to crawl right out of my body, I would come back to this place. As wonderful and powerful that image proved to be for me, the belief I created that day has grown so much bigger, so much better, benefitting me and my family and many individuals that I have been privileged to work with.

I believe that I can heal.

I believe that you can heal.

I believe we are created to heal. I believe healing is available. I believe healing is our destiny.

For every person healing happens in stages that are unique. I cannot slap a formula on my healing or yours, nor will I tell you how to heal in 3 steps, or 5, or 20. My heart's deepest desire for you is that you begin to believe that you CAN heal, that it is possible. I believe it is happening for you, even right now, at this moment. Inhale…exhale… Again, deeply, with intention and purpose.

While you *INHALE…* imagine all the divine healing power that exists in the universe being drawn toward you. Then as you EXHALE, release the healing power created by God woven in every strand of your DNA to bring light and healing to the world as it brings healing to you.

Practice this a few times then share a prayer of gratitude with me.

Abba, Father, thank you for creating me to heal. Thank you for creating me with healing power. I accept and receive healing with gratitude and generously share healing with others.
Amen.

I believe God to be a good parent. Jesus is recorded in Matthew 7:11 as stating, "If you, being evil, know how to give good gifts to your children, how much more does your heavenly father give what is good to those that ask Him." We pray for healing and hope for miracles and they happen! (In fact, I received a miraculous healing from endometriosis when I was 22, but that's another story.) However, healing doesn't always appear miraculous, just as a Savior doesn't always appear victorious. As of this writing, I am a parent of three children ages 12, 14, and 15. I love preparing meals for them that are nourishing and tasty. They (mostly) love it when I cook and bake for them. However, there are times when I say, "Darling, here is a pantry and a refrigerator full of delicious, healthy food. Why don't you make something that you will enjoy? I have provided the tools and ingredients for you. You have the ability and resources to create nourishment for yourself. Have fun and enjoy!" I think healing, whether needed in our body, our life or relationships is like this much of the time. We want God to provide a ready-cooked, prepared, instant healing miracle. Sometimes He does and it's wonderful! Many times, He points us in the direction of the kitchen with dozens of options, but we need to create with what He has given.

The road to healing is a ROAD. And it's not a day trip or meander down the lane, it's a road that takes everything. You must leave behind many dearly held beliefs and desperately held relationships. Traveling this road will change you. It must change you. If it doesn't, then it isn't a healing road to begin with. But, what it will give you! That is the stuff we endure in hopes of, our wildest imagination surpassed…

To create change, we need to do just that. Create. Create something new, a new feeling, a new experience.

Imagine wildly.

What would you do if you could do ANYTHING?

How would I want life to be if it could be anything?

If I could not fail, what would I do?

If I was always loved, who and how would I choose to love?

What if God is better than we can ever think or imagine, more pure, more good, more incomprehensibly loving, how would I feel about Spirit and the divine?

I discovered that if I approached life this way, asking myself these questions, I would do less things and enjoy more. I would give to others out of my overflow, without depriving myself or sacrificing because I know that I am enough and I have enough. I am not giving up anything. I am only being my truest self. Imagining wildly says "what IF…"

Every story has a beginning, a middle, and an end. The most important part of our story is the part we are telling ourselves right now, not the story others see especially through the magical social media lens, not the story others create about us, nor the one we tell others. The most important story is the one you are telling yourself, THAT is creating your reality. Sure, it started in the beginning. Your family of origin taught you how to think about life and yourself. But without change, you simply repeat whatever that was over and over. Our biggest battle is always going to be in the middle, when we are changing our story from what it was into what it will be. That is what I started that day on the bathroom floor. Fast-forward a few years, and I found myself kayaking on a sweet, sparkly lake, right outside the door of our lake house we had just moved into for the summer. I glided on the water flooded with awe over this completely unintentional manifestation. That is what imagining wildly will do!

I was right that day on the floor. It was just a chapter and not the end of my story. The end is yet to be written, but I imagine it's going to be amazing!

References:

To learn more about Dr. Robin Perry Braun and the Integrated Life Process, please visit: https://www.integratedlifestrategies.com.

Lipton, Bruce. *Biology of Belief: unleashing the power of consciousness, matter, and miracles.* Santa Rosa, CA. Mountain of Love/Elite Books. 2005.

The scripture reference was taken from The New International Version of the Bible.

MARY BETH VIEIRA

Mary Beth Vieira is a holistic practitioner and founder of Akarah Life Practice in Tulsa, Oklahoma. She holds a certification in the Integrated Life Process and is currently pursuing the designation Certified Naturopath. She happily makes a home with her family in Bixby, along with her lifelong partner and best friend, her three delightful, and sometimes challenging, children, one tiny white dog that thinks she owns the place, and a ginger tabby that actually does. Mary Beth loves living and celebrates everyday simple things like her morning walk and coffee with her husband on the patio. She finds purpose and incredible joy participating with her clients in their healing process, witnessing each beautiful transformation. This experience is the cornerstone of her mission and why she named her holistic practice after the Hebrew word "akarah" which was biblically used to describe a woman that had been barren but became fruitful. This name was spoken of her in advance, while she was in the midst of her shame, anticipating the favor that would manifest. Mary Beth feels this is also her story, that out of much darkness and pain she has also seen much triumph and become extraordinarily blessed. Mary Beth is excited to be an author and speaker, sharing her personal story and passionate belief that healing is for everyone.

Connect with Mary Beth at www.akarahlife.com.

Chapter 21

NEVER GIVE UP!

by Miss Marilyn

I started performing when I was six years old. All I ever wanted to do was to be a star, to perform in Las Vegas, and be in Hollywood movies. I believed I would eventually have my own talk show like Johnny Carson. That was my dream, and I was determined to make it happen.

When I was six years old, I was taught my first magic trick, and I immediately went to school and performed it on my teacher's desk for show and tell. My fellow students were flabbergasted, thus starting my love affair with magic and performing in front of audiences. I would perform one to eight times a week for most of my childhood. I attended more birthday parties in a weekend as a magician performing a 30-minute show than most children attend in their entire life. My mother drove me from party to party and sat in the driveway waiting for me. I performed all over St. Louis, Missouri, and the surrounding areas. I would compete in local magic shows and eventually go on to perform in New York and become the first girl to place at Tannen's Magic Camp annual competition. I would appear on the news in New York and my dreams would take off as I pursued a career as a magician and fire eater. I was going to have my own magic show on television and become an author in the future. By the tender age of 11, I was already speaking at events to adults about setting goals and crushing them. I was determined and talented. I was not encouraged by my extended family; they wanted me to go to collage (intentional spelling) and become a lawyer. My Nana, however, did whatever she could to support me, always. I never heard words like "follow your heart" or "do what makes you happy." However, I was self-motivated and nothing was going to stop me.

On June 5, 1998, first thing in the morning, my entire life would change. I would be "stopped." My dreams would be wiped away in about 30 seconds and I would be left attempting to deal with PTSD, health issues, to simply survive every day. I would quit driving, quit dreaming, and just focus on getting through the day. I was involved in an automobile accident that would take away my love, health, hopes, and dreams. This accident would leave me lifeless and alone. Daily survival was my focus.

I don't talk about this often and I am literally an open book. However, I have severe, debilitating fibromyalgia. It began in June 1998; I was at the precipice of an enormous career as a producer at a theme park and I was in the middle of pre-production in Hollywood on my own magic show on NBC. My dreams were coming to fruition! And in an instant, it was all taken away. My focus would become simply being able to get out of bed every day and use the restroom.

It was just the beginning of a nightmare I would call "my life" for almost 20 years.

And then in 2008 my C-section opened and it took a year to heal. My stomach was actually burned four times before my wound would close.

At one point, a nurse looked at me and said, "You need to come to grips with the fact this is how your life is going to be." I will never forget that moment. I was in diapers, in a nightgown, barely able to hold my head up, laying on the sofa, with an open wound in my stomach. I had not done anything in over six months but go from the sofa to the restroom.

Listen, I don't usually cuss, but I thought to myself, "Oh, hell no, lady. This is not how my life is going to be!" I was 37 with an infant and a 12-year-old. This "lifestyle" was not an option.

I already had debilitating fibromyalgia, which completely destroyed all of my hopes and dreams and now you think I'm not going to be able to walk at all. You think I am going to wear diapers full time and I'm just going to lay around … and I'm only 37 years old… hell no.

So, here I am in my nightgown laying on the sofa in pajamas and the nurse is gone. I had a choice to make, so I did the research and found out that they could burn my wound and hopefully it would heal. I didn't know it but, in that moment, I took over my "Second Chance!" I talked to a fabulous nurse practitioner and made the arrangements and right there on that same sofa after burning me four times, my stomach began to close and I didn't understand it at the time but… I found hope.

A few weeks after my wound healed, I decided I was going to walk again. But let me tell you, I was passing out at random any time I would stand up and attempt to take steps and would collapse and fall forward on my face. It was incredibly traumatic. And I seemed defeated. From performing on stages eating fire in six-inch heels in front of thousands of people, to not being able to walk to the bathroom four feet away without passing out. It was a nightmare I wasn't waking up from; I had been home almost a year.

Walking didn't really seem like it was in my future, but each day little by little over the course of a few years I got rid of the walker and the cane, and I was no longer in a wheelchair. And I walked.

Although I was on food stamps and Medicaid, I wanted to open a store where people could shop for free: and be treated like they were special and with respect. I wanted them to be able to pick out essentials and gifts for Christmas and anything they needed for their children. I'm leaving out a lot of details, but that's what I did, I opened up a store where you could shop for free, no questions asked, and you were treated like you were special. This element was extremely important to me because when you are not broke but dirt-poor people DO NOT treat you like you're special. And, I just felt like that was so wrong and every human being deserved feeling special. So, I opened Miss

SHE IS AN OVERCOMER

Marilyn's Second Chance literally on a prayer and $600. My son had received $600 for his 16th birthday and he let me borrow it to open the shop where folks in need could shop for free.

Within a year I was in a tremendous amount of new debt. However, I was also citizen of the year for my Acts of Kindness and I knew although it was not really working out, this was my calling. (I realize that last sentence didn't make sense... but that's faith.)

I looked for products to sell so that I could pay the rent and one day in the middle of the night when I was going to kill myself because I was just a shattered mother and nothing was working out for me, I accidentally found a five-dollar product. That night would dramatically change my life. Instead of killing myself, I became the most inspiring success story you are ever going to hear. I want you to understand after reading the story you can overcome anything and you can achieve the life of your dreams. No matter your circumstance, your relationship situation, the needs of your children, the needs of your aging parents, and especially if you are in your way. I am going to teach you that if you stop blocking your blessings, get out of your way, and decide that you are unstoppable and that you are going to Star In Your Own Life!, you will completely understand that you can do anything. You see, overcoming is a decision. On July 16, 2013, I decided not to kill myself and to take a leap of faith and to dare myself to live the life I have always dreamed of.

Is it easy?

No!

Do I regret the sacrifice and the tremendous amount of personal growth it took to get me here? No! I learned what the word HOPE means in the past nine years, I learned what the word faith means in the past nine years and, most importantly, I have learned what it means to serve others with grace. And by putting the focus on others I became the epitome of overcoming.

To be honest with you, I don't even think I knew what the word overcoming meant. The definition of Overcomer is:

over· com· er | \ ˌō-vər-ˈkə-mər\

plural overcomers

Definition of overcomer

: a person who <u>overcomes</u> something: one who succeeds in dealing with or gaining control of some problem or difficulty

... an advocate for women's rights, a voice for mental health awareness, an overcomer of drug addiction, a gracious celebrity ... who refused to be defined by any one of those things.

I had overcome many things in my life: my mother abandoned me, the death of my brother, being raised without a father, the death of a close friend, a rape survivor, a recovering alcoholic, and drug addict. Because of God's grace, I was able to conquer wanting to commit suicide and start a business. That can only happen with God. And once I realized I was living God's plan, I started hustling with him. I made a tremendous number of sacrifices, spent many nights on the ground sleeping at the flea market to get a spot, and did whatever it took to build the network to create an empire. Me, a chronically ill drop-out living God's plan for my life. It's faith over everything for me.

I simply do my best, every day.

To be honest, most of my life I thought I was God's practical joke. For example, all I ever wanted was a brother. When I was 18 years old my mother gave birth to the most beautiful baby boy you've ever seen. 47 days later, two weeks before Christmas, he died. In 2002, I fell madly in love with Prince Charming, the most wonderful man. We planned a fabulous wedding and were to be surrounded by everyone we loved. Six days before the wedding, he called it off. I was completely devastated; it was confirmed to me I was God's practical joke.

I could tell you story after story of things that didn't work out for me right before they were supposed to happen. I could tell you about tremendous heartache, sorrow and opportunities that never panned out. But I could also tell you stories that I now see happened in my favor. But at that time, I truly believed everyone else was meant to be loved and deserved wonderful things, except me.

The past nine years have been the best years of my life. I do Acts of Kindness daily, I have built a massive Empire based on serving others, I have become a multi-Seven Figure Earner in my industry simply doing my best, every day. I am, along with chronic illness and all, Paparazzi Accessories biggest success story. I have lived my own version of Cinderella (just add prince). By digging deep and leaning on God's Grace every day for the past nine years. I am now a mother to a son with special needs, an author, influencer, world traveler, speaker, philanthropist, and overcomer.

I am focused on my legacy and my legacy will be that no matter my health struggles, I created a movement of kindness and love. I am currently living in Southern Alabama building my dream retreat center on a hundred-acre farm where I found 'Destiny Pond' and I am growing pink lotus to symbolize Second Chances. No mud, no lotus is my mindset. I can find the beauty in any situation. My ministry is growing daily and I am extremely proud of my accomplishments. I have completely turned my life around by walking in faith and becoming unstoppable. I choose every day to live, "Star In My Own Life!"

I have built the life of my dreams, and I'm proud to say that I am an Overcomer. I dare you to dream as gigantic as you possibly can and never let anything stop you. Never give up. I am 51 years old. I have been through hell and back many times, and I am just now at peace with it. I feel as though my life is just getting started. I know there is a fabulous gentleman out there praying to meet someone like me and it will happen in God's timing. Do not let anything stop you from your hopes and dreams. Do not let anyone snatch them from you either.

I dare you! 💋

All my love

OX,

Miss Marilyn

MISS MARILYN

Miss Marilyn is a Bombshell, everyone's eccentric best friend, and a Hope Dealer. As a single mother of two sons, she has become a powerful example of a woman who never gives up on her dreams! She began her career at six years old with a love affair with magic. By the age of ten, she had pink business cards and performed magic shows all round St. Louis, Missouri. By high school, she became the only female comedy magician and fire eater in the world. She made it to the stages of Hollywood and in Las Vegas tragically caught on fire. Her passion and bright light would be dimmed as she struggled with continual adversities.

Destitute and suicidal in 2013, she is now a world-renowned life coach, and a pecan and lotus farmer. She designs prayer gardens, is renovating a 101-year-old building, and performs Acts of Kindness daily to spread love. She believes anyone can create their dream life if they simply never give up and continue to move forward in faith.

Miss Marilyn bought her company's starter kit as a dropout single mom with her last $300 while on the verge of suicide on the worst day of her life. From that, she created a powerhouse network marketing family of tens of thousands of hot pink feather boa-wearing members, The Blessed Bombshells, with her 13-year-old autistic son, Maveric, at her side. The Blessed Bombshells career sales in the last 5 years are over $200 million.

She is building her dream ministry with veterans and recovering addicts on a 100-acre farm in Southern Alabama. Miss Marilyn has appeared on several media outlets, including ABC, NBC, Inside Edition, Dr. Phil, and Good Morning America and is a social media trailblazer and an influencer who pioneered live selling.

Connect with Miss Marilyn at https://www.facebook.com/ BlessedBombshell.

Chapter 22

BUT, GOD!

by Mistie Layne

I've been referred to as the Empowerment and Resiliency expert because most people that know me can't believe I stay so positive after enduring one crisis after another. In my eyes, I'm just living life as it comes, getting through one day at a time. I am strong and have overcome a lot of obstacles, but I never did it alone. What does being resilient actually mean? It is being able to withstand or recover quickly. We all have LIFE happen to us with its tumultuous occurrences, but I have felt unusually burdened by adversity. However, my life hack to withstand it is to realize each time I survive through adversity, I gain knowledge, strength and perseverance to be better. I think of myself as a piece of art and God is the artist perfecting me to be my best. While I'm in the storm, I feel tired, resentful and fight depression and think I won't survive, **but God** promised to never give me more than I can handle, so I forge on. I stay positive because I know He is preening his artwork and I will be better on the survival side of adversity.

We all experience hardships from time to time and what may be a hardship for me, won't be for you and vice versa. I try and remind myself there are people who have it much worse in life than me, although it doesn't always help me in the moment. I share my story through speaking and writing to help others know they can not only survive after adversity, but they can thrive, too. When I learned to stop being the "victim" and instead used my experience to step up and speak out, I gave awareness and education so we could JUDGE less and

MENTOR more. I pray you, as the reader, find inspiration, knowledge, and compassion for others through my story.

I grew up spoiled and had a great childhood with a big house, swimming pool, dance and music lessons, and a stable home environment. I was on a mission to become a surgeon and worked hard to get to medical school. In college, I met my first husband and had two beautiful daughters, slowing down my plan, but I remained determined to fulfill my desire of medical school. Just when I was at the doorstep to becoming a surgeon, I found out my husband of ten years had another woman pregnant. I was so naïve and never even suspected he was cheating on me. I fell into a deep depression and felt it must be my fault. I was convinced I wasn't pretty enough, smart enough, good enough in bed, or whatever else I could blame myself for. Eventually, I began dating and starved for validation from anyone that I was good enough. I met Robbie and had no idea he would be the catalyst to my demise. I want to be clear before going forward to take full responsibility for my actions and decisions. Accountability and culpability are main ingredients to forgiveness of ourselves and surviving our adversity.

After dating almost a year, Robbie started avoiding me and not answering my calls for days at a time. I immediately took the blame again, thinking it was me and I just wasn't loveable, until I discovered his "mistress" was cocaine. I had no experience with drugs because after being hit by a drunk driver at 14 and almost dying, drugs and alcohol were never my scene. I was the good girl everyone expected to be a successful surgeon. However, I was in a place of vulnerability, dismay and depression over my marriage, and I didn't respect my moment of choice and tried cocaine for the first time. I was an educated thirty-two-year-old mother of two and should have known better, but I thrived on being bad for a change and became addicted very quickly to the escape the high provided me. My addiction very quickly progressed into a crack cocaine addiction, and I literally lost all power and control over my life. For ten years I teetered with crack, in and out of jail, doing all those things I said I would never do for drugs. I should have died with all the situations I put myself in, **but God** had other plans for me. I eventually gave into prostitution, and that led to rape and being held hostage at gunpoint, a volatile relationship where I was beaten black and blue and wanted to die, **but God** saved me through it for some reason, even though at times I wish I were dead because I was tired of hurting my family over and over behind my addiction. In transparency, my first felony was for stealing my then husband, Gene's, police undercover truck. I went on a mission and once I started smoking crack, I couldn't stop and go home. I had periods of time spanning 6-8 months at a time where I would be clean, then impulsively go back for one reason to escape or another.

Next came Joey, my dealer, who I married! He is the father of my son and the domestic abuse I endured with him has been the hardest to recover from. Our scars on the outside heal, but those buried deep within us can haunt us if we let them. During this chapter is where I sunk the deepest into my addiction, giving up on ever living a normal life again. I was convinced I was now property of the devil and couldn't be saved, **but God** had other plans for me. Sometimes we are saved in ways we don't realize. Bad things have a small silver lining to build on. Let me explain. I was attacked and robbed and when punched in the face, I lost control of my car and killed somebody that horrific day of September 18, 2007. I woke up in the ER with my mother sobbing over me and I reached up to hug her and tell her I was okay and then I felt the cold angry steel wrapped around my wrist. I knew I had been in a wreck but blacked out after. I never saw the woman standing in her yard, nor could I have stopped the car from sliding if I had..... nonetheless, she was gone and my mother is the one that had to tell me I had killed somebody. My gurney felt like quicksand, and I was sinking down feeling all the breath being squeezed from my lungs. Is this real? How did I get here from being a Miss Texas Teen runner up to hiding behind black eyes and now this?

I was snapped into reality quickly when I was given my arraignment papers and saw Vehicular Homicide-40 years!!! I was going from medical school to prison and felt guilty for being the survivor from the wreck. I dealt with depression and guilt while awaiting my fate. During the seven months it took to go to trial, I began my writing journey and tell people writing is the therapy that saved my life. I wrote all my pain, worries, anxieties, frustration and regrets down on paper and pen I bought from commissary. It took me seven long months, but I wrote my life story. The prosecutor heard of my book and visited me. He knew this wasn't my life and wanted to help me, not lock me away. My charge was reduced to Negligent Homicide, and I received the five-year maximum and off to prison I went.

After being released and finishing my parole, I quickly re-entered the medical field because God allowed me to keep my Nuclear Medicine license when the charge was reduced to a non-violent crime. I seem to be like a cat, always landing on my feet each time. I never published my story because I didn't want anyone to know about the old Mistie. I was ashamed of her, **but God** had other plans. He blessed me with my first grandbaby, Eliana, who was born on the exact same day as the wreck, September 18th. However, she got stuck in the birth canal and suffered a brain injury from lack of oxygen. Eliana was blind, deaf, couldn't suck or cry and never heard her daddy sing to her every night or saw her mother and the love in her eyes. Of course, I blamed myself. I let the devil convince me this was my punishment, there is no way the date is just a coincidence. Then, I remembered I learned in rehab that only 3% of crack addicts ever overcome their addiction and I was standing there 8 years later a proud 3%er! Eliana didn't have a voice, **but God** lit a fire in me to use mine. I re-wrote my book, *What Goes Up*, from a place of darkness and blame to a place of forgiveness and accountability and it became a best-seller. I never realized the process of transparency was healing me, **but God** did! I began realizing I was a survivor, no longer the victim, and I could actually use my experiences to help others. I began public speaking and started my company, Step Up and Speak Out. Eliana passed away in my daughter's arms when she was four and we were devastated, **but God** knew it was her time… Covid was right around the corner and we had just survived through a chemical plant explosion less than two miles from our homes and been displaced from the evacuation.

Right after Eliana passed, Covid hit and then we were hit back to back with two category 4 and 5 hurricanes. A tree fell through the roof of my daughter's house while we were in it and she was six months pregnant. She had to evacuate her home while being repaired from the explosion and now she is having to move again while pregnant. Like pollination happens routinely, I was being beaten down by chaos and trauma all around me. Furthermore, my parents' home was hit hard by both hurricanes and needed repair. I was overwhelmed with my own life and going through a divorce from another failed marriage! Life was happening and I was getting one blow after another. Two months after the hurricanes, we found out my mother had cancer and I had to move her in with me to get her through chemo. She beat the cancer, but Lewy Body Dementia and Parkinson's have taken over and she now permanently lives with me. Meanwhile, my stepdad was declining with his Dementia and I finally had to break down and move him in, too. I rented a large home for us and four months into our lease, the owners sold it out from under us. We had one month to get out and nothing available on the market to suit our needs. I finally broke down and bought a house, but again, was limited to what was available to fit their needs (both use walkers and can't have carpet). We moved three times in four months and that took its toll on all of us! My step-dad was admitted into the hospital for evaluation for his PTSD outbursts and came home with pneumonia, strep throat and a UTI. He went right back in the hospital and then to a rehab facility. Meanwhile, two weeks after we moved in, my A/C unit went out in the house during a Texas heat wave! Life is still "happening" to me, as it does to us all, **but God** stays true to his promise not to give me more than I can handle. God was there with me on the streets keeping me safe during my addiction. God was there for me keeping us safe when the tree fell through the house and God was there allowing me to keep my medical license so I would be able to care for my parents today. God saved me for a reason and I am on His mission now, not mine. I teach others to Step Up and Speak Out, either through writing or speaking. I also run Tween Esteem camps for 9- to 12-year-old girls to infuse them with confidence, self-esteem and teach them they can be resilient and use their problems to help others. I am passionate about teaching the youth today to be strong leaders of tomorrow.

I will continue to stay positive and remind myself I am strong and any adversity I go through, I now look at as education to help others. Examine your life and think about all the things you have endured and can help others with. When you think you just can't endure any more, remember, **but God** knows better and is sculpting you for something greater.

MISTIE LAYNE

Mistie Layne will inspire you with her courage to transparently share her journey which deemed her an empowerment and resiliency expert. She went from studying to be a surgeon to facing forty years in prison for killing somebody behind a horrific cocaine addiction. Mistie felt hopeless while drowning in her rock bottom continually punishing herself with toxic guilt and shame. She found the strength to pull herself up and claims writing was the therapy that saved her life. Her story will inspire you to overcome your worst to live your best by knowing we can ALL come out on the SURVIVAL side of adversity.

Buckle up to learn how your transformational journey to STEP UP AND SPEAK OUT will liberate you and help make a difference in the world. Mistie instills courage to STEP UP to your truth, the confidence to SPEAK OUT about it transparently and teaches you to conquer any adversity with resiliency. Her guidance puts you into action so your story today can save a life tomorrow!

Mistie is an international best-selling author, award winning keynote speaker, TV Host, and runs Tween Esteem camps for 9- to 12-year-old girls, teaching them about confidence, self-esteem, entrepreneurship and how to WRITE IT OUT when they need to release emotion. Mistie is writing *Action Takers Who Step Up and Speak Out* anthology book and is a contributing journalist for several international magazines. She practices Nuclear Medicine full time and serves as Vice President on the Chemo buddies 4 Life non-profit board of directors.

Connect with Mistie at www.stepupandspeakout.com.

Chapter 23

LIVING IN ABUNDANCE

by Naydia Mills

I remember that morning very well… the kids had been home from school for two weeks and I was baking biscuits. I never make biscuits, but the smell was intoxicating, filling every crack and corner with its southern goodness. When I opened the oven door, that hot heat hit me in the face like Georgia humidity at the end of June. One of my best friends got married in Georgia at that time, and I can tell you from personal experience, that kind of humidity will slide the icing right off your wedding cake.

I took the biscuits out of the oven, showed the kids how to mix butter and honey together, and then slathered that on a hot biscuit and took a bite. If you haven't figured it out by now, I'm a southern woman, born in Kentucky, but raised since I was two in the Tennessee Valley in a little town called Barren Plains. I was raised in a culture of pleasing and polite, yes sir and yes ma'ams were always expected, county fairs were one of the highlights of the year and love? Well, we served that up hot and bubbly in any number of nine by thirteen casserole dishes found in the cabinets of any proper southern woman's home. And it's there, behind those cabinet doors, that my story begins.

I spent a lot of time with my Grandmother Fanny. My Dad's mom was a hero of mine growing up. She made paper dolls with me, taught me how to make popcorn balls and fried apple pies, and wasn't afraid to ride rollercoasters in her 70s. She made me feel the most special. Growing up, whenever a holiday rolled around, we'd all show up at

Grandma's house to a spread of cheese laden, finger licking, home-cooking. It was in these moments that I learned to love others and myself, with food.

It's funny the identities we are given as kids. Several family members often called me "little Wanda," referring to my aunt who had always been heavier and had battled her weight for as long as I can remember. When I turned 14, I remember going to a doctor's appointment where I found out that I weighed 184 pounds. I was told that "something just had to be done about that," but I had no idea what that was. No one had ever explained what a healthy weight was, let alone why it was important for me. In the south, if something is bothering you, you'll likely be told to "git in there and git yourself something to eat." And that's exactly what I did... and that began my lifelong struggle with weight, health, less than great body image, and never feeling like I was quite good enough.

But the Lord had a plan in mind for my plus-sized story, He always does.

After I finished that biscuit, I remember having a conference call for work. I had scheduled a meeting with a potential client, and after having lost 60% of my business due to the onset of the 2020 pandemic, I was excited about the call. I took a selfie to document my excitement and quickly found myself disappointed in what I saw on the screen. I had been numbing my disappointment, anxiety and fear over my lost business and the stress of family pressures with food. I was cooking and baking my way through the pandemic, and ya'll, there was simply no denying the impact.

Later that week, while scrolling social media, I came across a statistic that approximately 40% of the individuals experiencing the worst impact from Covid-19 were obese, just like me. Reading that simple post took the breath right out of me. How would my poor health impact my family? What if I tried to get the weight off again? I had failed so many times, why would this time be any different? The patterns of yo-yo dieting swirled through my mind like the Tilt-a-Whirl® at the county fair circa 1998. I had failed at just about every major diet and weight loss fad that had been rolled out over the last two decades. Low carb, no carb, keto, personal trainers, point systems, shakes, pills, blood tests, allergy tests, thyroid tests, running, walking, fasting, cleansers, juices… quite frankly, the thought of trying again made me want to utter breathy cuss words that you could just barely understand like Grandma Fanny when she was mad but tryin' to be ladylike. So with the full expectation of failure and falling flat on my face, I reached out to a family member who had been sharing about her experience with her health coach. With potlucks on hold due to the pandemic, and birthday parties all having virtual themes, I assured myself I could fail in secret and no one would have to know. That single, terrified, step of faith would forever change my life.

The first time I spoke with my health coach, she asked me if failure wasn't an option, how much weight would I want to lose, and I laughed. I was 37 years old and had been at an unhealthy weight since I was 14, I had no idea what a healthy weight even was and even less confident that it was possible for me. Instead, I told her about the life I knew I didn't want anymore. I wrote down a few things on a scrap piece of paper laying on my desk, it still hangs in my office. Here's what I wrote:

- ➤ I don't want to hide in pictures anymore
- ➤ I don't want to look at jewelry or socks in stores that don't carry my size
- ➤ I don't want to cry in dressing rooms
- ➤ I don't want to tug on the front of my shirt
- ➤ I don't want to have anxiety about my airplane seatbelt
- ➤ I don't want my daughter to have to look for my belly button
- ➤ I don't want to feel self-conscious with my husband
- ➤ I don't want to look at weight restrictions on rides or activities
- ➤ I don't want to criticize myself and see only flaws when I look in the mirror

I'm pretty sure I cried multiple times writing that list, when I shared it and, let's be real, I cried just now writing those words out again. But it was the starting point for me, the crisis moment I needed.

I would be happy to share all the details of that first big chapter in my health journey and if you connect with me on social media, you'll see lots of posts that reflect my journey of losing over 100 pounds. It's a big, long trail of up and down, around and around, like an East Tennessee road in Appalachia, definitely not that single line from start to finish like my favorite chair lift in Gatlinburg. No, a health journey is anything but straight up. It's messy and hard, it will leave you with skinned knees and muddy shoes, tear-stained cheeks and bruised knuckles. But what you gain from pursuing health will far surpass the sacrifices required of you.

About three months into my health journey, I had lost over 30 pounds and I was sitting on my back patio with two girlfriends, a socially distanced mom's night out, flames flickering from the fire pit. We were all losing our minds and just knowing I wasn't going crazy alone was somehow helpful. This became a thing for a few of us. We even backed our minivans and SUVs into the parking lot and formed our own little kumbaya moment right there between Target® and Home Goods®. But that night on my back patio was different. Instead of desperation, fear and anxiety, I shared something new I was feeling – hope. I shared about how things had been changing for me and how I was excited about my health for the first time in my whole life. I was learning things I didn't even know about my own body, and I had a coach cheering me on! Later that night, my friend sent me a text, "I think I'd like to do what you're doing." I was ecstatic for her. "Sure," I said, "let me connect you with my coach!" There was a bit of a pause in our text conversation when this phrase came through, "Can you not coach me?" I literally remember laughing out loud. I said to myself and to her, "I am the last person in the world that should be coaching anyone about health. I've been unhealthy my whole life. Trust me, you don't want me doing this, you want to work with someone else." But despite my urging, she insisted she would rather talk to me. And much like the Lord does in His subtle and unexpected ways, He gently guided me forward into the purpose He had been creating for me for the past twenty years. Not only did He help me start to build words around this journey, but He gave me the strength to share it. I'm gonna tell ya, posting pictures in your bra and underwear ain't for the faint of heart, but my vulnerability gave that mom, that friend, that co-worker, even strangers, the confidence to have hope for their own health again. The Lord took that scary first step towards better health and turned it into a purpose and passion that I didn't know I needed or desired. Helping people find hope for health again has brought me more joy than those blue ribbons at the county fair when I was a kid. It's also changed the trajectory of my own family's health, how we talk about food, how we love each other, how we pursue healthy movement, what we see in others and how we love them, too. Only God could take that overweight, self-conscious 14-year-old girl and set her on a path to helping people lose hundreds of pounds, take back their health and regain hope for a better and brighter future.

When I think about what it means to be an overcomer, I go back to a word that has really been a common thread throughout my journey, abundance. I believe that Jesus came to earth to die so that we could have life and have it in abundance. As an overweight, unhealthy 37-year-old stressed out working mom and wife, I could not have honestly said I was living an abundant life. In a world where body positivity has often confused and encouraged us to neglect our own health, I feel compelled to remind folks that our body is a gift, and no matter its size, it's beautiful, worthy and has immense value. But the extra weight we carry around impacts our joints, our organs, makes us more susceptible to diseases and often prohibits us from experiencing the kind of freedom and joy that I believe Christ meant for us to have.

Being an overcomer might just mean taking a scared step forward into a health journey to embrace that you are worth the hard work it takes to be the best version of you that you can be, emotionally, mentally, and physically. That's what I now do every day as a health coach. I left my full-time job to pursue this passion of helping people discover the life they WANT, not just what they don't want. What if you could be your best self? What would that look like? How would it feel? What would you pursue? What dreams would you reach for? To me, being an overcomer means stepping forward, pushing through fear, and reaching for the life you want. Because it's possible. Everything we've been through, all the trials, all the hard, it has purpose because we do. If you learn anything from my crazy story, know this, that you can step forward into fear, embrace abundance, and choose to be an overcomer. I'll be cheering you on!

NAYDIA MILLS

 Naydia Mills is no stranger to success. Having worked in sales for over a decade, she is a driven high achiever with an incredible work ethic. After becoming a mom, navigating a traumatic birth and near-death experience, Naydia found herself at the height of her career, but at her lowest point in her health. Born and raised in the south, Naydia struggled with healthy habits and often turned to food for comfort. But at the onset of the 2020 pandemic, having lost most of her sales business and still grappling with finding identity and purpose outside of her career, Naydia began an unexpected health journey that changed the trajectory of her family, career and overall purpose in life. Naydia now serves as a health and wellness coach, helping clients lose weight, pursue healthy habits, and challenge their mindset to grow and pursue their best self.

Naydia has been married to her Jeff for 12 years and they have two kids, Elizabeth and Mason, and a golden doodle, Ginger. In her free time, Naydia loves to visit the beach, work out at Burn Bootcamp, walk, or bike the greenways, and she loves conversation time with fellow growth-minded moms and friends over coffee or a Target run. She also sings on the praise and worship team at her church. Naydia's ambition in life is to live a life of abundance!

Connect with Naydia at https://www.instagram.com/naydia_mills/.

Chapter 24

OVERCOMING THE TRAP OF PERFECTIONISM

by Pamela Lozano

From the time I was little, I was a rule-follower. Being raised as a pastor's kid and becoming a pastor myself in adulthood, I embraced the misconception that in order to lead well, I must be perfect. I aimed to lead by example, but failed to realize no one wants perfection as their goal, because it's just not attainable. But perfectly perfect was the standard I subconsciously aimed for most of my life.

I remember as a child having an innate ability to know right from wrong. As the oldest, I often bossed my younger sister around telling her what she should and shouldn't do. I grew up with strong convictions and saw everything through a lens of black and white. I didn't need a lot of correction, but had an inherent understanding of how to behave. I felt guilty when I misbehaved and often confessed on my own. In fifth grade, I cheated on a test and felt so guilty that when I got home, I immediately told my mom. She asked what I should do to make it right and I immediately decided to tell my teacher. Early the next morning before school, we met with my teacher who happened to also be the elementary principal, so I was pretty scared to admit the truth. But through tears and a shaky voice, I told him I had cheated. I still remember him shaking his head in disbelief. He was surprised at my honesty and because I confessed, he didn't punish me, but gave me a failing grade on the test for cheating. I felt a little better, but now needed to work harder to get my grade up. Again, perfection was the target, so I'd have to work hard to make my parents proud.

My parents never pressured me to make straight A's or "get the grade." I did that all on my own. They encouraged me to apply myself and do my best, but my desire to please them drove me to work hard to be my very best. While this may seem noble, it began a pattern of beliefs that I couldn't mess up or allow anyone to see weakness in me. I compared myself to the smartest students, prettiest girlfriends, most popular athletes and the most spiritual Christians I knew. I played the comparison game and never felt like I measured up.

We often look at the lives around us and compare, hope and wish we could have what we see. Social media portrays perfection of smiling faces, filtered images, and perfectly captured moments. But we forget these moments are only a slice of what's really happening in someone's life. Even though the image on screen looks amazing, the reality behind the lens is often chaotic and anything but perfect.

As a teenager, I had a beautiful friend named Jennifer. She and I were exact opposites. She was a brunette, tall, thin and athletic. I, on the other hand, was blonde, short, thin and not athletic at all. Jen was very outgoing and popular and always had the latest fashionable clothes. She knew just what to say and always had a crowd of boys dying to take her on a date. I had a small circle of close friends, wore hand-me-downs and wished for any boy to look in my direction. Our families were close, so we spent a lot of time together. I was so insecure around her because I constantly compared our lives. I felt inadequate because she seemed perfect in every way. We remained close until half-way through high school when my family moved out of town. Jen and I drifted apart and even though our friendship suffered, it was one of the best things that happened to me. For the first time as a teen, I embraced who I was and stopped comparing myself to others. I dove into singing and music and realized I had talents to be proud of; however, the perfection game continued.

Throughout high school and my young adult years, I behaved how I "thought I should act." As a pastor's kid, my actions reflected on my parents and I didn't want them to look bad. I suppressed my emotions and learned to be okay even when things weren't. I believed the lie that leaders didn't have a right to be upset when hurting. I learned to stuff my emotions and be who others needed me to be, rather than being true to myself. In order to be a good Christian, I thought my attitudes had to remain in check. I didn't have a right to be angry – because that was "wrong." Perfection was my standard.

At the young age of twenty-four, my husband and I became youth pastors at our local church. We were now responsible to spiritually lead middle and high school students. We developed a youth ministry, led weekly youth gatherings and events, and counseled teens through difficult situations. This created a new level of pressure for me because, now as a pastor, I was a role model to these young people and I couldn't fail them.

Things leveled out a bit in my thirties as I began to raise our children. I focused more on their needs and desires, but continued to set the bar pretty high. As a pastor, I began leading peer groups and had women of all ages looking to me for advice and input. They shared their lives with me and I began to realize authenticity was key. We shared life experiences and women leaned in as I communicated my mistakes. They were encouraged by the real and raw stories and I realized vulnerability bridges gaps and that perfection wasn't really attainable.

As my kids became teenagers, fear consumed me. I had heard so many stories of teens struggling emotionally and mentally. I was afraid they were going to fall into some of these traps and felt a deep need to protect them. I'd challenge their choice of friends and became a terrible listener. Fear became a motivating factor in everything and rather than hearing what they had to say, I'd cut them off and tell them what they needed to do. Instead of coaching them and teaching them how to grow up and make wise choices, I tried to do it for them. I demanded the "right way" all of the time and when they failed, it was met with a long lecture to try to get them to see things my way. There were no negotiations. Perfectionism now took on a whole new form as I tried to deflect my standards and convictions onto them.

As parents, it's important to know what season we are in. When little, our children need the constant instructions of how to do things in order to stay safe. As they grow older, we must learn to let go and teach them how to make decisions on their own, so when they become adults they have the skills to live life on their own. Making choices for them doesn't enable them to grow and learn. We must let go of fear of failing and allow them to learn from mistakes.

There was also a season in ministry where I became a less accessible leader. Because I didn't allow them to see my weaknesses, teens and young adults were not vulnerable with me. They hid insecurities and problems because they feared I would judge them. Perfectionism had unknowingly closed me off emotionally and I was unable to empathize. I often judged them for making mistakes, never outwardly, but secretly I was critical. Again, my inability to empathize restricted my ability to pastor at a deeper level, but I didn't know how to change because this was how I lived my entire life.

Things began to crumble when my daughter went through a really tough season in college. Being raised as a "PK," *she* now felt the pressure of perfectionism. She began an unhealthy relationship with a guy she knew wasn't good for her. She hid the relationship and denied it completely. Things spiraled quickly as she lived a double life – one where things looked good in front of us and another to please this guy. Her grades suffered and she lost a lot of weight. Her behavior changed as anxiety filled her life. She didn't want to disappoint us, but kept spinning the truth to stay out of trouble. I so badly wanted to believe everything was okay, but deep down I knew it wasn't. Worry filled my days, and at night I tossed in bed and woke up with knots in my stomach. At times I didn't even want to get out of bed. Things felt like they were spinning out of my control and I didn't want to face it. I didn't know how to help her and felt so helpless and alone.

My husband and I prayed and tried to communicate with her, but she was so defensive. Several months went by and, finally, the truth came out when someone read messages between them. Because I felt betrayed and really scared of how this would look, I got angry and confronted her. She was upset and sorry for the mess she'd made, but finally confessed to the pressure she'd secretly been living under for years. She felt confined and restricted all of the time, afraid to make a wrong move because of how I'd react or feel. She decided since she couldn't live up to my expectations, she'd just do whatever felt good in the moment.

My heart was broken and I felt like a complete failure. Here I was a pastor and mentor to many young women, and my relationship with my daughter was broken. My desire for perfection had become more important than her heart and well-being. I cared more about what others thought than the unrealistic standards I put on her, and the scariest part was I didn't know how to fix it. By the grace of God, things did change and our relationship is stronger than ever. But it didn't happen overnight, little by little things began to shift inside of me. I needed to change in order for things to be better between us.

I took a course with some friends that helped me see how I lived my entire life performing for others. It was always about "being on" and doing what I thought others expected from me. But as I dug deeper, I found I never allowed myself to feel deeply. My homework was to process my true feelings when things happened and ask why I felt that way. It was honestly brand new for me to sit with my feelings and try to understand what was going on inside. Why did I care so much about what others thought? I discovered it was because I was afraid that I was not lovable. Why was I so insecure when I made a mistake? Because I was afraid that I wasn't enough. Why did I feel left out when I wasn't invited to go out with my friends? Because I believed I couldn't be a good enough friend. On and on the list went. I believed lies about myself, so I tried to perform and be "good enough" to feel better about myself. What a life-changing revelation!

As I began to untangle these lies and sit with truth that I learned my entire life, peace filled my heart. I no longer had the pressure to be perfect. I could embrace my weaknesses and be okay with not being good at everything. I realized I need others to fully be alive and that their strengths added so much to my life. This changed my entire way of thinking and freed me to be a much better mom, a more secure wife, an empathetic pastor and a better friend. I'm still on this imperfect journey, but I'm now able to embrace it and be okay with this imperfect version of me.

PAMELA LOZANO

Pamela Lozano is the Founder and President of Pure Design Ministries – a 501(c)(3) non-profit organization that empowers teen and young adult women in self-image, self-worth and pure beauty. Pure Design embraces, encourages, equips and empowers young women through social media, magazine publications, photoshoots, devotionals, conferences, church events, and mentorship and ambassador programs.

Pamela leads a Girl Boss Network of young female entrepreneurs to coach, mentor and strategize their business dreams. She has written and facilitates a Mom2Mom Power Hour which is an online mentorship course for moms of teen and young adult daughters. She has been in youth ministry for over twenty years and loves counseling and pastoring young women. Pamela also currently works as Next Gen Pastor with her husband Jake at their local church in Columbus, Ohio.

Pamela is passionate about empowering girls with truth and loves to speak to women of all ages, but particularly teens and young adults. She loves spending time and serving with her three amazing kids – Caeilen, who co-founded Pure Design, Judah and Markus. She loves shopping, decorating, Mexican food, and Starbucks® peppermint hot chocolates. Future dreams include launching a foundation for young women to help launch their business dreams.

Connect with Pamela at www.puredesigngirl.com.

Chapter 25

PIGEONS DON'T HAVE MIRRORS

by Sally Larkin Green

As soon as Jesus was baptized, he went up out of the water. At that moment heaven opened up and he saw the Spirit of God descending like a dove and alighting on him. Matthew 3:16

I was about to turn 30 and was working full time while selling cosmetics part time at night. However, all my hard work seemed for nothing. I felt like every time I worked towards something, it was taken away from me.

I had prayed so hard for a child. On my birthday in December of 1992, I was sitting in the office of the cosmetic company I worked for. I was trying really hard to act happy, while feeling so sad and dead inside. I wondered where God was and why my life never seemed to go the way I wanted it to. I was depressed and knew if I kept going in this direction it wouldn't be long before I would be in a downward spiral and wouldn't be able to lift myself out. The next day I woke up and looked in the mirror. I didn't recognize the woman staring back; I certainly didn't like her. I was so frustrated, overwhelmed, and angry. My prayers didn't seem to be getting answered.

Earlier that year, in the summer of 1992, my husband and I decided to put an addition on our house. It was a very small house and there was no room to start a family. We were both working and had saved up some money. We heard an advertisement on the radio for a new home construction company. They were advertising prefabricated additions where they would do all the work in their factory and assemble the addition at your home. We contacted the company and one of the representatives came out and gave us an estimate. We were so excited. They drew up the plans and the job was going to cost a little over $40,000. We went to the bank and secured a second mortgage and hired the company to begin as soon as possible.

We gave them one third of the money up front for supplies and were told they were going to begin construction at their factory. They were very good at communicating at first; however, they kept moving the start date of the construction out two or three weeks every time we called. When they finally came, they cut into our deck, brought in a backhoe, and dug six huge holes in our yard and poured sonotubes for the foundation. Then they delivered some wood for the walls. We were going to have a living room, bedroom, and half bath. We were so excited.

They asked us for another one-third payment and told us they were almost done. They showed us invoices for the windows and flooring they had purchased that they were holding in their factory. My husband and I went out and ordered all new kitchen cabinets and furniture for the new rooms. We stored it all in my in-law's basement until the addition was done. The construction was supposed to start in a couple weeks. The day came and went, but nobody showed up. We called and were told they had backlogs on other jobs and the weather was an issue. We waited two more weeks and again they never showed up. We called again and they pushed our start date out a few more weeks.

One afternoon we came home and there was a sheriff in our driveway. He gave us paperwork stating that the company we had hired to do the work was filing bankruptcy. We were devastated. In total we were set to lose over $30,000. All our dreams were smashed to pieces. I was so angry. I felt stupid for trusting the salesmen that had promised me a new addition to our house; I was devastated at the thought of losing all that money. When my husband said that maybe this was a sign we shouldn't have children, I completely lost it. So here we were, in this small house, we had just lost $30,000, our marriage was strained, and my prayers, again, didn't seem to be getting answered. We were paying on a mortgage every month for an addition we didn't have and every month when I wrote that check I felt like I was going to throw up. I wanted to sell the house and move, but my husband loved the little house and didn't want to move. We had a little over $10,000 left from the loan plus some money we had saved. I cried a lot, prayed a lot, and thought a lot.

After that, I didn't care. I didn't care about my job, how I looked, or what the house looked like. I stopped selling cosmetics and began to eat my feelings. I started gaining weight, and I still didn't care.

One Sunday while I was driving to church, I was stopped at a red light. I looked over at a flock of pigeons on the grass. One of them stood out from the rest. He was bright white. Here he was the only white pigeon in a flock of blue-gray birds. I looked at him and thought, I wonder if he knows he's different? I wonder if he feels out of place like I do? Then I smiled to myself and thought, don't be silly. Pigeons don't have mirrors. He probably doesn't even know he's different.

I continued driving to church and when I got there I had completely forgotten about the birds. I was a Sunday School teacher and I loved teaching the kids. I would always get there about an hour early to set up my Sunday School classroom and get my weekly lesson plans from the church school superintendent. She handed me the lesson plan for that week and I sat down to review it. It was the story about the baptism of Jesus. I shared the story with the kids and we made origami birds. If you remember the story, when Jesus got baptized God sent a dove out over the sky afterwards. One of the girls handed me her little origami bird and said, "Here Miss Sally, this is for you, I want you to have it." As I was driving home from church, I passed the spot where I had seen the pigeons earlier. They were gone and I wondered where the white pigeon was. And I looked over on the seat of my car and there was a little white origami bird from church. Suddenly it hit me like a ton of bricks. That could not have been a coincidence! I knew instantly that God was with me, that God was hearing me, and I knew that everything was going to be okay.

After that, I decided that I was going to make the best of my situation. I was going to step into my greatness. I started listening to motivational tapes again. I had gone to see Tony Robbins a few years earlier and I had purchased his personal power program on cassette tapes – yes, cassette tapes! I started listening to them again. I started eating healthier and learning how to shift my thoughts. I started to read books, so many books. Books have always been my escape. It was my escape when I was younger and it is my escape to this day. I started my self-help journey. I read books like *Think and Grow Rich* by Napoleon Hill, *The Seven Habits of Highly Effective People* by Stephen Covey, *Unlimited Power* by Tony Robbins, and more. I made a vision board and I wrote down everything that I wanted to happen. We received $10,000 back from a government fund. With that money and the money we still had, we were able to put a small addition on our house. We expanded our kitchen, added a living room and laundry area. Then, a few weeks before I turned 31, I bought a pregnancy test and the results were positive. I wasn't sure how my husband would react, so I wrote him a note inside a card, sealed it, and left it for him on the kitchen table. When he opened it and read it, he was sooo excited.

We all go through struggles and setbacks. By having faith, taking action even when we don't feel like it, and being open and noticing those "winks" from God, we are able to grow spiritually. It's our struggles that help us gather the strength and determination we need on this rollercoaster journey called "Life." One of my outlets, in addition to reading books, was writing poetry. Enjoy this poem I wrote called, "White Dove"

WHITE DOVE—POEM

by Sally Larkin Green

When you wake up sad and lonely,
and you want to cocoon in a ball and scream,
When there's no song in your heart anymore,
and you're falling apart at the seams,
When butterflies glide through the air,
and when the white dove soars,
I'll be there.

When the stress of everyday living creeps up,
and you're just holding on by a thread,
When every day seems like a chore,
and you're facing each day with dread,
When butterflies glide through the air,
and when the white dove soars,
I'll be there.

When you wake up with joy in your heart,
When the person you love holds your hand,
When your child takes their first steps,
and everything's going as planned,
When butterflies glide through the air,
and when the white dove soars,
I'll be there.

SALLY LARKIN GREEN

 Sally Larkin Green is the Creative Director at Action Takers Publishing. Their mission is to empower 5 million women and men to share their stories with the world to make a greater impact on the planet. Action Takers Publishing specializes in themed anthology/ collaboration books where each writer contributes a chapter. They also publish solo books.

Sally is a 6-time International Bestselling Author and is currently in the process of writing her own book titled *The Self-Care Rockstar* due to launch January of 2023.

In her spare time, Sally enjoys painting. She teaches acrylic paint classes to local senior centers, women's groups and children's summer camps.

She is a mentor helping women to grow spiritually and her Self-Care Rockstar program helps women begin and continue their self-care journey.

Connect with Sally at https://actiontakerspublishing.com.

Chapter 26

SHE'S BETTER AFTER IT ALL

by Sheba Empowers

It was October 1, 2017, when I heard these words: "I hate you." Never imagining that I would ever find myself in this place, I knew in my deepest parts that my family will never come back together. The vows that were spoken did not endure, "Till death do we part." I asked myself, till death, do we part? Or how is it that some people have what seemed to be the touch? This magical touch that allows them to enjoy bliss and happiness with the one who is the peanut butter to their jelly or ice to their cream. Unfortunately, that is not the case for everyone. Many couples experience the generational curse that plagues a lot of families: DIVORCE.

I would boldly rephrase that and say, DEATH. My marriage died. Not one of my CPR trainings could help me ever bring it back to life again.

Those words, "I hate you," were spoken to me by the one person who I would give my life for, my son. I know he did not know what that meant, but it still broke me into what seemed to be one million pieces. I thought to myself as I attempted to cope or even shield from anything else he may have said, "He could not possibly hate his first love, after all, I know his heartbeat and he knows mine." Either way, his real truth or perceived truth pierced my heart like a knife. I promised myself that I would not cry in that moment, but you better believe when I returned to my friend's home, on her cold leather couch, I would definitely let out the water works. Speaking about that, I cried a lot on that couch. I never imagined living with someone, sleeping on their couch and living out of two solid suitcases. No one would have been able to convince me of it; nevertheless, it was my life.

I was broken and destroyed.

What happens when the strong person needs to be strengthened?

Living in a new reality and facing all of my fears was daunting.

I am a pretty ambitious woman. Over the course of my living in North Carolina, I rented two apartments on my own, so it is not like I have not done this before, but it was different this time. I actually do not mind being alone, but this time I was alone, if you know what I mean.

Not knowing what was to come, one thing I did know is that I had to move forward. I also knew that it would be a process; this was my new norm. Sometimes I question my strength. I ask myself if I am in denial, because I have always been good at redirecting negative energy. I would be the first to admit that I do not hide it. Trust me, my apartment walls have heard deep moans and groans. Additionally, my sheets and comforters have absorbed many tears and snot...oops! My close circle listened to extensive phone calls and read many text messages at all sorts of times at night or in the early morning hours.

The focus has always been on accepting reality and moving forward, regardless of how long that may take.

What seemed like a spiral going downhill in my personal life, the opposite was true in my professional life. Over the course of two years, I received two major promotions. Both initiated by the company. I put on my face. I showed up no matter what. Being the youngest Director in a 13-location organization and given the branch with the most unreputable reputation, to say the least, was no easy feat. I did my absolute best to change the reputation of my center, and I was successful.

I had my cheerleaders cheering me on. No one knew what was happening, but they genuinely wanted me to succeed in all of my endeavors. Suddenly, I hit rock bottom in my emotions. More and more people began to put the pieces together. I had to rely on what I do best, redirect negative energy. One thing for sure is that I would never allow myself to wallow in self-pity. That was a no-no! I would not allow it.

I turned to God. I turned to sisterhood.

Chatting with a friend led me to discover that I had to start a women's group. I remember telling her that I knew it had to have a significant name with meaning if I was going to invest in it. In that moment, I remember my abdomen area literally feeling like bubbles or water. I do not know how to even describe it, but what I do know is that something was moving on the inside of me.

Ever since I was a young child, I always preferred to go through things so that others would not have to. I've come to discover that the strength I possess has to be SUPERNATURAL.

From that place, SHEBA it is!

I sat on it for about 24 hours. The name triggered my natural curiosity. I began to read up on this mysterious woman, 'Queen of Sheba,' and even checked out a few YouTube® clips about the infamous Queen of Sheba. This quest for information led to article after article and video after video. The information centered around Christian and Muslim beliefs; both giving very similar accounts, except her origin. Although I am a very highly spiritual person, I did not want to focus on the origin because I thought it would be a means of division rather than unity. Thus, I merely focused on what she represented.

Queen of Sheba is famous for paying King Solomon a visit after hearing about his limitless wisdom. She wanted to inquire and probe his mind. Reading about her made me see myself; fearless and bold, definitely an unorthodox type of a woman. She was driven and determined. She knew what she wanted and went to great lengths to see to it that it happened. May I also mention, she got the King. If that is not power, then I do not know what is.

My thoughts began to race. I felt so connected to this 'mystery' woman. Then, it hit me like a ton of bricks. SHE'S BETTER AFTER IT ALL, no wait, (SHE)s(B)etter(A)fteritall. Ah! That is better.

There was an immediate shift in my mindset and life. I did not want people to even know my story; I wanted them to know my strength. Was it a secret? Absolutely not! However, I find that oftentimes we spend too much time focusing on our downs and we find ourselves staying down. I knew that the greatest message that I would ever be able to tell is not the words spoken over a microphone or during an interview, rather, how I live my life.

People needed to connect with life while experiencing life. That was my mission. That was my goal. I wanted every woman to discover that through it all, SHE'S BETTER AFTER IT ALL. From that moment forward, I became 'Sheba.' It is to the point that I do not think anyone calls me my actual name anymore. However, I will never complain because it brings me great joy. I earned my badge. I cried my tears in silence, but I also rose up from the ashes. In essence, others watched me rise up from the ashes and then discovered my story. I cannot say that I actually had that as part of the plan; it just seemed to happen that way.

Someone once asked me, what is it? What is the key to overcoming and moving forward?

The key is giving up control to gain control of the only person you can actually control, which is yourself. Wishing and hoping, praying and dreaming will never change things that are simply not meant to be. Accept it.

I often tell people that purpose is fulfilling a need. I do not see it as being a magical moment that happens. Purpose is discovered by living even if that living is in the trenches but rising up like a phoenix. What need does 'Sheba' fulfill? Sheba allows women to understand and operate in their power. Women need to know this. As mentioned, they need to know by seeing other women live it.

Since beginning Sheba, my life has taken on a new meaning. There is not a day that goes by that I do not think about how I can be a better and more productive woman. Doing so adds more value to the mission and purpose of 'Sheba.' It starts and ends with me. It starts and ends with you. It is no one else's responsibility to make sure your life counts. I started my consultant business: Sheba Consults LLC, published my first children's book: *Heart of Gold* and have been privileged to be the guest speaker at many events and podcast interviews. Might I add, I am remarried and have two beautiful twin girls. I am blessed! No one can convince me of anything else.

When I turned to God in my darkest hour, He responded by giving me His light. I have connected to so many people who I feel pull what is in me out of me. There is no such thing as going backwards. Too many people are relying on me to continue to be a beacon of light and even hope or joy.

I live and love with no regrets.

Sheba Women's Empowerment group started with a person, but will finish with a legacy.

MRS. EMPOWERMENT QUEEN

Mrs. Empowerment Queen, Sheba is the Founder of Sheba Consults LLC and SHEBA Women's Empowerment group, which stands for She is Better After it ALL. Born to empower women and children/youth, Sheba has been groomed from "A born leader" to "a GREAT leader," serving as a mentor to others.

In concert with mentoring, Sheba educates. Simply put, she believes "To empower is to educate," and she interweaves this principle in every area of her life. As such, Sheba is an Early Childhood Educator & Consultant, Career Advisor, Professional Development Specialist and Grant Writer. She also takes great pride in being a public speaker and author.

Connect with Sheba at www.shebaempowers.com.

Chapter 27

BUT GOD...

by Shelly Snitko

Storms! Whether caused by nature or life's challenges, each of us can expect to encounter some stormy weather. If you haven't already, you will. Storms in life are inevitable, as certain as the sunrise. I wish we could claim a free pass, but at some point, no matter who you are or how hard you try, adversity and heartbreak will upset the rhythm of your life. Storms crash into our lives without discriminating or showing favoritism. Rarely are they welcome. They often strike when we least expect them, without warning. Families, marriages, friendship, and careers are all affected as we deal with the storms' aftermath.

Here in the southern part of the United States, we are well-acquainted with storms. Thunderstorms, tornados, and hurricanes blow in and out often. On April 27, 2011, two extreme weather fronts collided creating dangerously unstable conditions in the atmosphere producing the "perfect storm." An outbreak of over 216 tornados unleashed waves of destruction across our home state of Alabama. For eighteen long hours we stayed "weather aware" as tornado sirens sounded throughout the day. We often took shelter in a closet under a staircase in our home because we had not yet purchased an official storm shelter. It was a day like none I had ever experienced. I was completely terrified as an EF-5 tornado passed less than a mile from our home. Later I discovered it had been on the ground for over two hours and carved a 132-mile path of destruction!

Chris and I have been married for over 38 years, weathering our fair share of storms. But in 1993, a storm outbreak, much like the tornados of 2011, ripped through our life. Storm after storm descended upon us, pushing us to the brink. Neither of us thought we'd survive the constant blows seeking to tear apart our family. Besides the normal challenges of two working parents raising two young children, my mom was diagnosed with breast cancer. I spent the next two years traveling long distance trying to help care for her as she battled it until her premature death at the age of only 55. Still grieving her death, I discovered my husband was having an affair with a co-worker. Sadly, this was not his first infidelity. But this time he was determined to end our 10-year marriage and completely disrupt our family. Regrettably, after the first affair, we never sought counseling. In our ignorance and pride, we simply tried to pick up the broken pieces and move on. The deeper issues in our marriage continued to fester beneath the surface. The "perfect storm" was unleashing its fury and I felt powerless to stop it.

To say I was blindsided would be an understatement. I was completely shattered. Bitter and angry, I felt like a bystander in my own life as I watched it unravel. Now what? How could I keep going without the two people I relied upon most? They were my anchors. To be completely honest, I didn't think life was worth living without them, but I had two small children depending on me. The thought of single parenting terrified me. I no longer had the energy to "be tough and power through." This was too much to bear.

Weariness and overwhelm were my constant companions. My entire life I tried to control things as if somehow I could protect myself from harm. I took pride in being seen as a strong, determined woman. None of that mattered now. Look where my self-reliance had gotten me!

In this lonely, desolate, and desperate place, I could hear a still small voice say, "Shelly, come to me!"

I thought, "Did I really hear that?" "Lord, is that you? I've really made a mess of everything."

Again, I hear, "Shelly, come to me! Are you ready to let go and surrender your life to me? Stop thinking you need to control everything.

You can't! I know this is too much for you, but this is not too much for me. Stop running! Come to me. Nothing is impossible for me!"

In that moment, alone, in a puddle of tears and heartbreak, I did!

I cried out, "Yes Lord! I surrender…I trust you with my life. Please help me. I cannot do this alone. I need you!"

I wish I could say everything magically changed. It didn't! Chris and I separated. What did change was ME! My constant companions were no longer hopelessness and overwhelm. I had peace! I hadn't realized it before, but I never had peace! Yet, in that moment and the days, weeks, and months that followed, His peace was my lifeline, my steady and sure anchor during the storm.

Every day there were challenges. Questions to wrestle with. Why me? Why my family? Why her? How could this be happening? Why now? What's wrong with me that he doesn't love me anymore? What did I ever do to deserve this? But I learned to release the answers to these questions to God. I chose to cling to His promises instead. Little by little, moment by moment, I absorbed myself in the truth of God's word. My trust in God's plan grew. I consistently surrendered my desperate attempts to control things. Eventually, Chris and I did seek biblical counseling. Neither of us had an expectation our marriage could be reconciled, but we had our children to consider, and they mattered to both of us.

We couldn't see or comprehend it at the time, but God, the master restorer, was already restoring us and our marriage!

1 Peter 5:10 assures us of God's promise of restoration and hope when everything around us screams otherwise.

"And the God of all grace, who called you to His eternal glory in Christ, after you have suffered a little while, will Himself restore you and make you strong, firm, and steadfast." (NIV)

Webster's Revised Unabridged Dictionary defines the verb "restore"
…

to bring back to its former state; to bring back from a state of ruin; to repair; to renew; to recover.

To fully grasp the significance of God's promise of restoration, you need to look back a few verses. There's a necessary posture required (vs. 6) to receive the blessing God intends.

"Humble yourselves, therefore, under God's mighty hand, that he may lift you up in due time."

Don't miss this! Humility, not pride, is necessary. Amid the storms and challenges, we often tend to try harder or think we need to do more, but God is telling us, no! Stop trying to be tough and carry on in your own strength. There's a different way, a better way, but first you need to lay down your pride. Reconciliation and restoration is not a do-it-yourself project.

Another key point is that restoration doesn't happen without resistance. Notice verse 8, God warns us to expect a fight. We have an enemy and he is not going to relent in trying to take you down.

"Be alert…your enemy the devil prowls around like a roaring lion looking for someone to devour. Resist him!"

Week after week, month after month, we saw the counselor, hoping to rebuild from the ruins. Trust me, we felt every bit of the battle. I remember so many times wanting to quit, but I leaned into the promises of these passages. God desired to restore; the enemy sought to destroy.

In partnership with the Spirit, the counselor began unpacking my pain, anger, and bitterness not just from within the marriage, but we journeyed into my childhood as well. Unaware, I had harbored years of woundedness because of my dad's alcoholism…heartache my family never talked about. In fact, my mom discouraged it. I can still hear her saying, "it's not right to air our dirty laundry" (it's likely that she had learned that from her childhood, too).

Over the years, I became an expert appearing one way, while numbing my pain and hiding behind the "perfect family" façade. But I couldn't escape the truth. Things weren't as they seemed. I lived alone in a silent prison. I hid the anguish and shame caused by years of sexual abuse, a secret my dad insisted I keep. Year after year I buried the pain deeper and deeper. In my desperate attempts to feel secure, I tried to control everything (and everyone). I built walls of self-protection around my heart unconsciously keeping others at arms-length so I wouldn't be hurt by them. A series of dysfunctional relationships and date rape merely perpetuated my unhealthy way of surviving the trauma. When I met Chris, he seemed so different than any of the guys I knew. I began opening myself up to him. I trusted him fully. It was like a fairytale; I was the damsel-in-distress, he was my knight in shining armor…that is until his betrayal!

But God, being rich in mercy, because of the great love with which he loved us, even when we were dead in our trespasses, made us alive together with Christ. Ephesians 2:4

BUT GOD!

Two simple but powerful words.

But God saw behind the smile that covered up the deep hurts.

But God saw the brokenness and woundedness from childhood pain which left me feeling like a lost cause, ashamed, and worthless.

But God knew my controlling nature, self-reliance, and self-protection were responses to having been a victim of sexual abuse.

But God was the only one who could rebuild, heal brokenness, bind up old wounds that had been neglected.

But God used the "perfect storm" I thought would destroy me, my marriage, and my family to redeem us.

Amidst the rubble of conflict and the chaos of emotional destruction, God gave the storm purpose!

It was during the storm he changed everything including the foundation upon which we built. Up until now, we had lived the life of the foolish builder referenced in Matthew 7 who built his house on the sand...

"The rain came down, the streams rose, and the winds blew and beat against that house, and it fell with a great crash."

We had built our life on a sandy foundation. It was weak, shallow, insecure, unable to hold up under pressure. Going forward would require a new one. We spent one long year of deconstructing the old and building upon new, but God restored our marriage!

He has been rewriting our beautiful love story ever since. Together, we purpose to keep Him in His rightful place in our hearts with Christ as our firm foundation.

In hindsight, we can see how God always had a purpose for our "perfect storm." In the words of Fern Bernstein, "Only God can turn a mess into a message, a test into a testimony, a trial into a triumph, and a victim into a victor."

Every storm and hard lesson learned prepares us for what lies ahead. Our experience taught us that no matter the size of the storm, the challenges we face, or the hardships that test the foundation of our faith, one thing we know for certain,

---

"Unless the Lord builds the house, those who build it labor in vain."
Psalm 127:1 ESV

SHELLY SNITKO

Shelly Snitko has been married to her college sweetheart, Chris Snitko, for 39 years and is blessed with 2 adult children, a son-in-love, and 4 grandsons. Together, they are creating a life we love here in Alabama.

She is a business owner, wife, mom, nana, caregiver, friend, and mentor who understands the many roles and daily demands on women. Her role as a family caregiver for their adult son with physical disabilities over 26 years provides her with personal experience navigating challenging life circumstances, loss, disappointment, and the ever-changing responsibilities associated with caring for a loved one. As women, we often find ourselves busy caring for others but guilty of neglecting our own self-care. Caregivers notoriously struggle in this area, often excusing and ignoring it. Shelly has moved from a place of surviving to thriving by reclaiming her own health and wellbeing. She understands that caring for me too isn't me first, but it means prioritizing self so that you are better equipped to manage stress and the inevitable disappointments we face daily. As a health coach and the founder of Caring For Me Too (a faith-based health and wellness community), Shelly's passion is to help other women prioritize their health. With authenticity and vulnerability, she uplifts, inspires, encourages, and supports others toward whole health so they, too, can flourish.

Connect with Shelly at https://www.facebook.com/shelly.snitko.

Chapter 28

HEART CENTERED HAVOC

by Sherri Leopold

In 2013, I began to have fluttering in my heart. It was very noticeable when I laid down at night. I saw my doctor. He said he couldn't hear anything specific, but he referred me to a heart doctor. The frequency had increased; it was never painful, it just felt weird.

After seeing the heart doctor several times and wearing a heart monitor, once for 48 hours, and again for 30 days, the data was inconclusive. He concluded that I needed to stop drinking Diet Coke®, eating chocolate, and I needed more exercise. My heart would still skip occasionally. I was 48 years old. Fast forward two years, and I encountered the biggest obstacle I could have ever dreamed of. I was betrayed by my own heart, or so I thought. I was extremely busy working multiple jobs, volunteering, and sitting on the local city council. I was also the lone chairwoman of a city festival which required hundreds of hours of planning. I had incredible stress during this time. I realize, looking back to that time, that my heart was speaking to me, but I wasn't listening. It was trying to tell me that I wasn't respecting myself. Chaos was brewing inside, and I just kept pushing myself. I ignored the warning signals in my body and kept pushing to do what everyone else wanted. I needed to execute what I had committed to.

In late 2014, after serving for almost 4 years on the local city council, I reapplied to run again. I did so at the urging of others on the council. I enjoyed my time serving, but wanted to be done as I wanted to move to a larger town. I ran again, even though it wasn't what **I** wanted. First lesson learned in becoming an overcomer; listen to your own intuition and heart center. Because I didn't, I piled on more to overcome.

During the campaign, I endured what I would call personal harassment and character assassination. I lived, volunteered, and served in that community for 20 years. My husband and I raised three children there during. None of my service mattered. The thousands of hours I donated to the community didn't matter. My voting record didn't matter. It was made personal.

As I was publicly torn apart via social media, the local newspaper, and at the local coffee shops, I was emotionally devastated. I had political signs that I paid for that someone was either outright stealing or laying them flat on the ground so you couldn't see them. It was becoming apparent that I was going to need far more than myself to navigate this.

At first, I tried to still attend church. The pastor was very wishy-washy. He couldn't support me as he felt that meant taking sides. I just wanted prayers. This was too much to ask for. My faith in the church itself was falling apart. I had people who served with me on committees look right at me and look away. My husband and I made the decision to not attend, after 17 years there. In hindsight, it was a very important step in my own spiritual growth. It's where I began to take responsibility for my own spiritual health by learning to cultivate a personal relationship with my God.

As I was searching scriptures for strength, I came upon this scripture in Ephesians.

Finally, be strong in the Lord and in his mighty power.[11] Put on the full armor of God, so that you can take your stand against the devil's schemes.[12] For our struggle is not against flesh and blood, but against the rulers, against the authorities, against the powers of this dark world and against the spiritual forces of evil in the heavenly realms.[13] Therefore put on the full armor of God, so that when the day of evil comes, you may be able to stand your ground, and after you have done everything, to stand.
Ephesians 6:10-13 NIV

This became my comfort. As I continued to have my family maligned online, my service and character questioned, I kept repeating to myself that I was protected by the Armor of God. With that armor on, I began to make decisions for my future. A month before the election, I decided I was no longer going to live there. Regardless of the outcome of the election, I wanted to move away. I let my husband know I could no longer live there, and he could come with me or not, but I was going. Yes, it was a bold statement, but one based and rooted in self-preservation. I was positive I was destined for a greater purpose than I was able to serve being in that small town.

I lost the election, and I was so grateful for the loss. A month before the election, my husband and I had already begun searching for a new home 30 minutes away. We had already detached ourselves from the town, our church, and our lives as a part of that community for the past 20 years. The house where we raised our children was up for sale. There was no lack of traumatic feelings.

In May, just a few days before my 50th birthday, even more chaos appeared. I had eaten spicy sausage pizza for lunch and was watching a television show with my daughter who was home from college for the summer. I thought the pizza had given me heartburn. I tried every conceivable remedy. Absolutely nothing I used worked at all. It just burned all night long. I couldn't sleep. I Googled® everything. The symptoms kept pointing back to my heart. I promised myself I would go to the doctor in the morning if my chest was still burning. It was.

I made an appointment, and they took me right away. My blood pressure was as high as it had ever been, and the EKG machine came rolling in. The nurse practitioner said, "Congratulations! You have just earned a ride in the ambulance. You are going to the hospital."

I haven't ever been in the hospital, except to have three children. All the things I needed to figure out are whirling in my head. Who needs to be called, who's going to watch the animals; what is wrong with me?! In less than five minutes, I am on the gurney headed to the hospital. The EMT took my blood pressure, and it is now 30 points higher than before. He gives me a Nitro tablet under my tongue. He asks me about two minutes later to rate my pain.

ZERO.

I am now acutely aware that this isn't a possible thing, It IS the thing. My heart is malfunctioning, and I am not even 50 years old. As we roll into the emergency department, people are running everywhere.

How did I get here? I just kept repeating it in my head. How did I get here? Why is my heart betraying me like this? I was nice. I helped people in this community. I volunteered, and I worked so hard to make a difference. Here I am lying flat on my back in an emergency room after my first ambulance ride, praying to God Almighty that I hadn't had a full-blown heart attack. Yet, there go all my clothes in every direction, everyone talking at once, and everyone is running and working with great urgency. Their haste made me more nervous than what was happening. I am grateful for their attentiveness, but it didn't help alleviate the fear. I wasn't in any pain at all. Maybe I was dying, and I was unaware. They informed me that they were going to do a heart catheter. They wanted to check to see if I had had a heart attack.

The heart doctor who was on call in the ER said, "Have you had any major stress, a death of a spouse or loved one recently?" I asked if character assassination counted. He laughed and said, "Maybe, if that is stressful to you."

Well, stressful wasn't even close to covering it. He went on to explain that I had what was called "Broken Heart Syndrome." This is typically seen in much older couples who have been married forever and suddenly one passes and the other one dies of a "broken heart." I didn't have a heart attack BUT my heart was, in fact, talking to me.

I started listening...and talking back.

My heart was warning me that I was letting the stress get to me. I ignored the warnings that had begun two years earlier. My heart doctor likely missed the importance of the symptoms that started two years before because of my age. I was only 48, and not something you typically EVER see in someone that age.

I overcome this obstacle of heart-centered havoc by learning to communicate with my heart. After spending my 50th birthday stuck in a hospital, I vowed I would never ignore my body again. I am acutely aware when my stress level goes up now. When I left the hospital, I was terrified.

In the three weeks that followed, we packed our house of 20 years, spent seven days on a long-planned vacation in Florida, and then moved into a new house. It wasn't stress free for sure. I spent so many nights following this event, lying in bed, feeling twinges, or small aches or squeezes, and I could feel the panic beginning to rise.

I questioned myself two to four nights per week; should I wake my husband and go to the hospital? I felt like I didn't know what was just uncomfortable versus something terrible. This was the beginning of my journey of talking directly to my heart. This conversation strengthened my personal relationship with God as well as allowing me to feel in control of my body. I would have daily and nightly conversations on what my heart's job was. I told my heart that I needed it to be strong, cooperate, and empty the chamber fully and strongly. If I felt any fear rising, I would repeat over and over, "I am strong" and "I am healthy." I also expressed gratitude several times a day for serving me. I still do. Because I AM one with God, I felt quite confident that together we could overcome.

I have a much better relationship these days with God, and my heart, too. No problems of any significance for the last seven years. I am happier and healthier than ever.

People often overlook the power of our mind. Our actions follow our thoughts. If we are worrying, our body serves up something to worry about.

I am still very heart centered. However, now I am intentionally mindful of my relationships, how and with whom I spend my time. This allows me the space to remain calm if I disagree with someone. I can freely agree to have a different opinion without the slightest urge to get them to side with me. I am simply present. Present with my conversations, with my body, and clear about how I will treat it. In turn, it will treat me well.

I feel as a nurturer we can always run the risk of heart-centered havoc. My heart centeredness almost cost me my health. When I put on the Armor of God and walked hand in hand with the Holy Spirit, all was well. No more heart-centered havoc for me.

I will always lead with my whole heart, but I now listen when it speaks to me.

SHERRI LEOPOLD

Sherri Leopold is the Leader of the Stop Self- Bullying Movement, Mentor, Author, Speaker, CEO of Dream Big with Sherri Leopold and Option Creators.

Sherri has authored 10 books including 8 International Bestselling books. She loves working and collaborating with others. She is a licensed Dr. Amen Brain Trainer and teaches on better brain health.

She's worked in the Network Marketing/Direct Selling industry for 25 years, sharing her expertise in speaking, mentoring, and team building. She has earned 31 incentive trips in those 25 years. She is focused on helping people find options to create the life they love. She is a 200K Leader with Le-Vel and has developed a thriving community of leaders. Sherri also hosts the television show Outside the Box with Sherri Leopold on Legrity Media TV. She loves shining a light on other servant leaders who are making a difference in the world.

Sherri resides in Springfield, Illinois, USA where she is passionate about encouraging others to live the life they deserve and Stand UP and Stand OUT as the unrepeatable Miracle they are!

Connect with Sherri at https://sherrileopold.com/.

Chapter 29

I WILL ALWAYS BE SICK

by Stephanie Suzette Caldwell

I had been diagnosed with bipolar disorder with auditory hallucinations, generalized anxiety disorder, premenstrual mood dysphoric disorder, acid reflux, and seasonal allergies. I was taking two different mood stabilizers, an antipsychotic medication for sleep, prescription strength heartburn medicine, and allergy medicine. I believed the lie that I would *always be sick*.

Of course it didn't start there. My mom had my sister at 17. She had me two years later and then my brother 18 months after that. My mom and dad got divorced when I was 4. After their divorce, my dad rarely paid child support. My mom worked a job or two and went to college classes full time. She struggled a lot with mental illness. My mom did seek help, but life doesn't stop when you are trying to get better.

It all started when I was 9 and I explained it as "my heart hurts." And my stomach hurt, too, All.The.Time. I purposely did not tell my mom right away. My mom was in bed a lot, so depressed she couldn't move. This got a little better with time and when she was married to my stepdad when I was 7 or 8. I felt bad for feeling bad.

It did get bad enough for me to mention it to my stepdad. Eventually my mom got involved and took me to the doctor. I drank a radiocontrast agent while they watched using an x-ray. Afterwards, the doctor told my mom it looked like "little volcanoes going off everywhere" spewing acid inside my stomach. They prescribed me acid reflux medicine and it got a lot better. Afterwards, they determined it was induced by stress and constant worrying.

I worried so much about *everything*. I worried we didn't have enough money because we didn't most of the time. I worried the electricity was going to get cut off because it did frequently. I worried my mom was going to get sick again because it still happened. I worried I wasn't doing enough because there was always so much left to be done. I worried my brother and sister were making my mom's life harder because they did. I worried no one liked me at school because I was made fun of and was in the slow reading group. At 13, I was diagnosed with generalized anxiety disorder and depression. I was prescribed an antidepressant and continued therapy.

When I was 18, my first daughter was born. I had *some* postpartum depression. However, it was nothing like after my second daughter 3 and 1/2 years later. There were a lot of contributing factors: the stress of moving to Alabama, living with Jason's (my now husband) family, working two jobs, having a toddler, my pre-existing depression and anxiety, just having had a baby, and being in my early 20s. Over the next four months, I began cycling through mania and depression. I had never been manic before, so I didn't know what to call it other than "I feel crazy." I was in so much emotional pain that it was unbearable and I couldn't talk to anyone about it other than my psychiatrist. I was too depressed to kill myself right before I checked myself into a psychiatric hospital, where I was for 10 days.

A few months later, my mom called. She was having trouble getting out of bed, getting things done, going to work, and so forth. She asked me if I could come back to Tennessee for a week or two to help her. It was already a month into college, I had a job, and two small children. My hands were tied, so I told her I couldn't. Because she was sick, this is the rest of the conversation:

Mom: [straightforward and serious] Do you ever feel sad and depressed anymore? Do you still think of killing yourself?

Me: [really thrown off and not sure how to answer those questions but being honest] Yeah, sometimes.

Mom: Well, you might as well kill yourself because you're never going to get better. You're going to be just like me and you will always be sick.

Me: [slightly light-headed and struggling to come up with words] Mom, you, uh, you don't really mean that. You're going to get better. I'm doing better now. I can come at Thanksgiving; that's not that far away.

Mom: We'll see. You don't know what it's like. None of your children are willing to help you and everyone has left you all by yourself...

Afterwards, I stuffed that deep down until it came up in therapy eight years later. After a few more months, it was apparent that living in Alabama was no longer healthy for neither Jason's growing addiction problem (I found out later) nor my mental health. After my semester was over, we moved back to Tennessee. The next fall, Jason told me he was addicted to opiate pain killers and had been spending all of our money on it. He would be in and out of rehabs over the next couple of years. The first intake counselor suggested I attend Al-Anon®, which is for friends and family members of addicts. When he would get out, I thought I could help keep him sober if I just didn't put too much on his plate and continued to shoulder all of our family's responsibilities.

Over the next year, I left him, he escalated to shooting up heroin and stealing, and I quit letting him see our girls. We found him an open bed at a detox facility and he left his phone with me. A text came through from the mother of a woman Jason worked with. This was the gist of her text, "I can't believe you're not man enough to take care of your own child. You have a daughter with my daughter and you're gonna step up or I'm gonna make you..." Jason had another child... a daughter... with another woman. Even though we weren't together when she had the baby, we were together when she got pregnant. After getting out of a 90-day rehab following his detox, we had organically gotten back together, despite finding out about his affair and the baby.

That November, I became sick again and was having suicidal ideations. I only stayed three days in the psych hospital this time, but they did tack on an additional diagnosis: premenstrual mood dysphoric disorder. That's really crazy, no pun intended, that my mental stability wasn't *as* affected as before. Was I getting used to tragedy? Was I becoming immune to pain and heartache? Most days I just felt numb and began to not really *feel* anything at all.

The following spring, I was sick again. I started counting my Klonopin®, but I wasn't going to have enough to kill myself. I'm not sure if Jason heard the clinking of the pills in the bottle or if it was a divine voice, but something told him to check on me. He drew some pretty accurate conclusions and with a weepy voice asked me what I was doing. I tried to play it off for about two seconds before I told him I didn't have enough to kill myself and he didn't need to worry. We immediately packed my bag and went to the ER. I went to a psych facility for almost a week.

In May, I accepted a teaching position and started in August. I slept less, worked more, and was still bad at asking for help. I spent most every Saturday and Sunday working at school. One Sunday night, another biology teacher texted me asking if I had found what she had left for me. I responded with, "I didn't go up there. I haven't been feeling well. Having a hard time handling my life right now lol." This is after having the year from hell: adjusting to having an *additional* one-year-old daughter, most mornings taking three kids to three different places before going to work, having a freshly sober partner, being overworked and underpaid, all the while my mental health is deteriorating and spiraling out of control.

That night, I knew I was going to kill myself. My plan was to take some Klonopin® just to ease my nerves, write a suicide note, and then overdose on Lithium. I began writing my suicide note. First to my girls, telling them none of this was their fault and they should never blame themselves and they were better off without me and so on. The combination of the depression, the crying, and the Klonopin® made me pass out asleep on the floor before I was finished writing.

I woke up and realized what had happened. I wasted those Klonopin® and wasn't going to have the courage to do it. I started swallowing as many pills as possible while everyone was rushing around getting ready for school. Jason realized I wasn't getting ready for work and saw the empty pill bottle. He said he was calling an ambulance. I knew I wasn't dead yet, so I ran to the bathroom and started swallowing random pills since he was distracted. While still on the phone with the 911 operator, Jason grabbed me from behind and pried the pills from my hands. I started blacking out and was in and out of consciousness.

I stayed in the Critical Care Unit for three days. Afterwards, I was transported to a psychiatric hospital. My stay was six days. After seeing how many times I had been hospitalized, five times in the last four years, the doctor suggested an outpatient partial hospitalization program. It would last for three to four weeks Monday through Friday during the day. I agreed to go.

Soon after, I went back to my weekly Al-Anon® meetings. I shared what all had happened. One member, Joe, had previously shared he had prostate cancer. Through the healing power of Jesus, his friend Rex had led Joe through his healing and he was now clear of any cancer. Joe asked if I would be willing to meet with Rex. The problem was, I didn't believe in God or Jesus or any higher power for that matter. I was an atheist, but I agreed. I knew I had nothing to lose. I was *going* to try to kill myself again. I felt utterly hopeless and figured I would try anything at this point. I was at rock bottom and had nowhere to look but up.

After our second meeting, I was ready to be all in. I accepted Jesus Christ as my savior, prayed for healing, and believed with all my heart that I was healed. From the life altering to the seemingly mundane,

SHE IS AN OVERCOMER

He healed "every kind of disease and illness... he healed them all."
(Matthew 4:23-24.)

A mustard seed of faith is all it takes... we've all heard that before.
(Matthew 17:20.) But there is another side to that coin: you also have
to have no doubt or unbelief. You have 2 cups: belief and doubt. You
can have one single drop (the mustard seed) in the belief cup and that
is enough to move mountains. But if you have *any* in the doubt cup, it
doesn't matter how much you believe. Jesus tells us, "I tell you the truth,
you can say to this mountain, 'May you be lifted up and thrown into
the sea,' and it will happen. But <u>you must really believe</u> it will happen
<u>and</u> have no doubt in your heart." (Mark 11:23 NLT, emphasis added.)

When you've lost all hope, when you feel all alone, when you feel
like there is nothing left for you, all that's left is faith. I believe it was
easier to accept my miraculous healing because there was nothing left
for me. I had nothing left to give, but could only receive. That's what
true grace is. Undeserved and not earned.

STEPHANIE SUZETTE CALDWELL

This chapter is a condensed version of a chapter from Stephanie Suzette Caldwell's full-length book *Despite it All...*

Despite growing up surrounded by mental illness and eventually being diagnosed with multiple mental and physical illnesses and being told she will always be sick, Stephanie has persevered, overcame, and is now doing very well. Despite being an atheist, she found Jesus and is working towards becoming a fully devoted follower of Christ. Despite growing up in poverty in a single parent household where coming home to the lights being cut off was just a normal Tuesday and then marrying into an almost identical family, she is now debt free (other than those pesky student loans). Despite getting pregnant at 17 and again at 21 with a partner who-would-later-be an addict, she still graduated *Cum Laude* with a double major in Biology and Chemistry and a minor in secondary education. Despite the drugs, the affair, and the subsequent child, she decided to stay and continue to love her now husband. Despite it all, she is still here and still remains hopeful.

Connect with Stephanie at https://sites.google.com/view/despiteitall/home.

Chapter 30

I HAVE A VOICE

by Tanquer Dyer

Have you ever been molested or sexually assaulted by someone close to you? It's a memory and a pain that I will always remember.

As a child, I remember staying on Lexington Circle. I can picture the old corner store where we bought the penny bubblegum, the 10 cent candies, Now and Later®, Lemonheads®, Boston Baked Beans®, and Chico Sticks®, and of course, the 25-cent dill pickle. The neighborhood looked rundown. From the corner, I could see the apartments my aunt used to live in. I had some really good memories there: playing on the merry-go-round at the park, play Ms. Pac-Man® at the Laundromat, sliding down the stairs, playing jacks, playing in her closet on the steps, and waking up on Saturday mornings to Betty Wright's "No Pain, No Gain" while we cleaned up.

I also remember my room on Lexington Circle. I had bunk beds and the first dreadful memory started when I was about seven or eight years old around the 3rd grade. I was going to Vollentine Elementary. I didn't hear my stepfather come in and he managed to get behind the head of my bunk bed. I don't know how, because the bed seemed close to the wall. What I do know is that I woke up to my stepfather rubbing my 7- or 8-year-old hands on something. I couldn't see because he was behind me. I asked what he was doing. He said, "Nothing. Go back to sleep." At the time, I didn't know what had just happened or what my hands were touching. It wasn't until later that I realized it was his penis that he had my hands rubbing on.

Some time had gone by, but he soon started back, coming in my room, lifting my blanket. I remember when my cousin came over, we slept in the living room on a pallet on the floor in front of the square fan. I could never really sleep because I was afraid my stepfather would come. Sure enough, even while my cousin was there, he would lift up the ends of the blankets trying to look at us. I remember asking what he was looking for and he said it looked like we were hot.

I remember as a little girl, I used to crawl into bed to talk to my mother, but then would he get in the bed, too, and started touching me. So I stopped getting in the bed with my mommy whenever he was around. I can recall him sitting me on his lap one day. He said, "You I know I love you, right?" I said, "Yes." He said, "You know it's ok for daddies to see their little girls, right?" I said, "No." He said, "You're growing up and I just want to see my little girl growing up." He asked me if I would let him see me and I said no and went to my room and closed the door. I didn't come out until my mother came home, which seemed like an eternity.

I remember times we would be in the car picking up my mom from work and he would say, "Let's practice writing." He would write things like, big and hairy. I had no clue what he was talking about at the time. I can recall times when he would write messages on the countertop in the kitchen when we lived on Winchester like, "Why you won't let me see it? Why you being stingy?" I wish we had iPhones then so I could take a picture of it and show it to my mom. When my mom came home, I would race to the kitchen, but he would always erase it before she came home.

We moved from Lexington Circle to a house near Ford Road. New house, new scenery, new changes… well, something never changes. I would try to stay up all night until he went to bed. I know God kept me, because I would somehow wake up while he had the blanket up. I would start moving to make him think I was getting up. He would try to get in a corner of my room as if I didn't see him standing there. I guess since he was so dark-skinned, he thought I couldn't see him.

The next morning, I would pay for it, though. He had to drive me to Snowden Junior High since it was so far away. On the way to school, he would call me stingy for not letting him look at me or touch me. I would ask him why he was calling me stingy and he would respond, "You know." I hated to be late for school and he knew it. In a Ford Mustang, he would drive EXTREMELY slow. By the time I got to school, I was so frustrated and upset.

As I got older, I locked my door. When we moved into the townhouse on Winchester, he put holes in the bathroom door so that he could watch me while I took a bath or shower. I remember telling my mother and she told me to put toothpaste at the door. I would stuff towels under the bathroom door and put toothpaste in the holes so he wouldn't look at me.

I remember the last time he touched me. I had moved back home right after I graduated from Christian Brothers University. My room was downstairs and I would lock the door directly to my bedroom. There was a guest bathroom downstairs with a sliding door that you could use to enter my room. I remember telling my mom that the door would not lock for some reason, but I would keep it closed. He came through the bathroom and slid the door open while I was sleeping. I remember waking up to the feel of someone touching and feeling my vagina. I screamed. At least I thought I was screaming... my mouth was open, I was yelling for my mom, but nothing came out of my mouth. I jumped up and he ran out the door. I told my mother and, even then, he lied. I packed up some things that night and left the house forever.

As a child, I constantly had the same dream. I was about 6 or 7 years old and running in the woods. My hair was long and straight, like I had gotten it pressed for Easter. I had on a long dress and all I remember seeing were trees, no houses, stores, or buildings. While I was running, I was crying and looking back, hoping that whomever I was running from wouldn't find me. I could never see the person. I just knew that I had to run. I would run until I got to the same tree every time, the tallest tree in the woods. I would get on the side of the tree where I felt like no one could see me and slide down the tree quietly. I would bring my knees to my chest and hold my head down between my knees until I fell asleep in my dream. The dreams went away, but the pain was still there.

I don't think anyone has any idea of how much hurt and pain I felt from being molested by the one person I called Dad. I don't think anyone knew the pain I felt from not having a father to love me, guide me, protect me, cherish me, hold me, play with me, sing with me, fight with me, or tell me that I'm his princess. Being molested left me broken. I would hear them describe me as smart, beautiful, an awesome speaker, organized, giving, kind-hearted. They didn't know that inside, I felt weak, scared, ugly, unattractive, and found it difficult to trust anyone. No one would ever believe I frequently had low self-esteem and felt lonely. As a child, I don't remember a lot of good times. I suppressed so much and sometimes feel like I was robbed of my childhood.

Being molested left me in a state of constantly trying to prove my worth, working hard not to feel the emptiness. I felt like I always had to protect myself because I didn't have a father to protect me. Because my mother knew about the molestation, I also didn't feel like I had a mother to protect me. I was left feeling vulnerable so many times. In college, there was a time I didn't care about myself at all and had moments of promiscuity.

It wasn't until I had my own daughter that I realized how scarred I was. I remember watching my husband with her and silently being afraid he would try to touch her. It was a struggle to get the thoughts out of my head because of what I had gone through. When my daughter was older and asked what it was like as a child, I didn't have a lot of stories because I had suppressed so much—the good and the bad.

True healing began when God brought this lady into my life, a teacher I had while I was working on my Masters for Marriage and Family Therapy. I was sitting in class and it was the second day of lessons. This lady knew nothing about me. We were talking about the need to recognize your biases and vulnerabilities in order to be a better therapist. Out of the blue, she walked up to me and put her finger on my shoulder and said, "Tell the little girl that's sitting here on your shoulder that she is safe. Tell her that she no longer has to be afraid and you don't have to protect her anymore. The dreams you had of running, you no longer have to run. You're safe now." I broke down in the middle of the whole class, a room full of strangers, and just cried. In just a few sentences, God had spoken to my very heart and He broke the chains I didn't even realize I had.

From that day, God began speaking to me in my readings and showed me that everything I thought I had missed out on, I really didn't. He said, "I told you I would never leave you nor forsake you, and I didn't." He began to show me that I wasn't fatherless because he had always been a father to me. He began to show me that he had placed men in my life when I needed to be fathered like my Uncle Arthur. Uncle Arthur showed me what it was like to be protected, guided, and teased as a pure father during the time I stayed at their home. He helped me with my homework. Even as an adult, he would give me words of wisdom and even washed my car.

God said you were never alone because "I was with you every step of the way." I began going to counseling and my counselor she just happened to be a Christian. She said, "I normally wouldn't do this, but do you mind if we pray?" and she prayed a peace that comforted me like no other. God had given me a peace that truly surpassed all understanding. The more I talked about the things I had gone through, the more my childhood memories came back. The more I read the Word of God, the more he showed me who I was. The imperfect image I had of myself became perfect. I realized I was created in the image of God and everything that I went through was not all bad. It had taught me to be strong, independent, and vocal. By feeling like I wasn't heard as a child, I grew to be determined to be heard, to become the voice of the voiceless.

TANQUER DYER

Tanquer Dyer served as a Captain in the United States Air Force. During her career, she served as a Protocol Officer, Chief, Military Equal Opportunity, and Section Commander, 820th Security Forces Group.

After her career in the military, Tanquer struggled to find her purpose as a civilian outside of the military. It was her own personal misery that catapulted her mission and ministry. Her pain gave life to her purpose and destiny of transformation. Despite challenges and obstacles, Tanquer received her M.B.A. in Human Resource Management and M.S. in Marriage and Family Counseling/Therapy.

Tanquer has had to adjust and make the necessary moves and transitions with her family through 3 overseas assignments and 10 different bases due to her husband, at the time, still being on active duty.

As a proud mother, veteran, and having served as a military spouse, Tanquer understands all too well the demands of the military and the challenges of deployments, TDYs, reintegration, relationship stressors, family changes, raising children (TEENS), spiritual concerns, refocusing, goal shifting, prioritizing SELF, work/family balance, and LIFE in general. Tanquer's desire is to help others see setbacks as setups, to see obstacles as opportunities, and to see devastation as divine roadmaps to destiny. Tanquer is committed to being a voice of encouragement and accountability and committed to teaching supportive skills that will lead to clarity, confidence, and courage to reach your full potential mentally, physically, emotionally, financially, and spiritually.

Connect with Tanquer at Tanquerd@gmail.com.

Chapter 31

TIME TO LET GO

by Teresa Dawn Johnson

I made a decision at the age of 24 that, I didn't know at the time, would affect the rest of my life and the future of my children. The decision was to marry their father. I had numerous signs that this probably wasn't the best relationship for either one of us yet, because we were pregnant with my first born, we decided that we would get married. We had only known each other for four short months when we got married in October 1994.

The first five years of our marriage was what I call hell on earth. When I was pregnant with our youngest, the situation caused us to take a look at the problem. The problem was more than alcoholism; it was alcoholism and everything surrounding alcoholism. The problem was never one thing; it was everything and no one way to define exactly what it was.

My spouse got help for his problems and I sought help for my problems. We were working our programs individually, but something still wasn't working. After four separations, we decided to work on us together. To be utterly and completely honest, I was scared. When the truth came out that he was with another woman during our separation, I felt completely wronged. I was angry and I wanted to punish him.

Today, I understand that my feelings are my own and that he was not responsible for my anger. It was how I chose to deal with the situation that caused my anger. I was so angry that that anger was killing me inside, killing my spirit. A friend recommended that I go to anger management classes. Because I was in the pit of my despair and at my lowest point, I truly wanted to feel better. So, I agreed to go to.

During that time, I understood the cycle of anger and remorse as well as my part in it. After the classes, I was in individual counseling with the leader of the class. Then the counselor invited my spouse to talk things out. Not only was he an alcoholic, but he also had bipolar. I knew from my recovery that I can only be responsible for me; I can only change me. The only time change comes from the other person is when they want to make the change for themselves. He decided he did not want to take medication for bipolar and that was his decision. For the next six weeks, our relationship declined even more rapidly.

Over the years of our 13-year marriage, what has meant the most to me is my church family, my involvement with the women's Bible study and ministry at my church, and my co-dependent recovery program. After another emotionally painful argument with my spouse, I went to my bedroom and shut the door. I got down on my knees at the foot of my bed with my face in the blanket sobbing praying to God for guidance on what to do. Then I sat there quiet with no thoughts, hoping for an answer. The Holy Spirit spoke to me, "It is time to let go. You have done all you can. You can do no more. It is time to take care of you and your two sons. I will not leave you. I know you know this misery and do not know being single. I will take care of you."

I knew that I couldn't tell my spouse to leave, so I continued on the best I could. I started to notice my spouse didn't come home almost three or four nights a week. Unfortunately, at this point he was not doing well either. Then one day he called and said that he wasn't coming back home. I asked him when he was coming to get his stuff. He said he would pick it up when I was not there.

I sought a divorce attorney. With the investment to the attorney for the divorce, it was also an investment in myself and my two sons; an investment in my unknown future. I was placing my life in God's hands. I was turning my will and my life over to the care of Jesus. Although

I had a bachelor's degree, I could not walk into a job without job experience. I knew clerical work quite well, so I worked for temporary employment agencies.

A wonderful woman who taught an all-ladies Sunday school class at my church had come alongside me in my marriage journey with the togetherness and separations. She voiced her observations to me. She let me know that she could tell by my facial expressions when my former spouse was in the home and when he was not. She said I smiled more and was pleasant when he wasn't home and had a look of grief and sadness when he was present in the home. She was a retired insurance agent. She recommended that I call around in our area for agents that might have an open position. She said that the work was mainly clerical and that it would provide more stability than going from one temporary job to another.

I took her recommendation and called insurance agents in the area to see who may have a job opening. I found a woman agent who was waiting on a training agent to move out on his own. After four months, I started working there. I took the exams for my property and casualty insurance license. It was shortly thereafter that she decided to fold her business and go back to her corporate job with the insurance carrier. I found a job with another agent a little closer to my home and had a shorter commute. Three weeks later, the second agent let me know that she would need to let me go. She assured me I had done everything right, but an outside decision was made, and she had no control over it. I was unemployed for two months and then got a job near my home. Not only did I no longer have a commute, but if I needed to leave for the request of my oldest son's teacher to run a quick errand, I was granted that ability. I had seen God's hand in this journey as I worked closer to home. I did not plan it nor would I have thought of it. It was God's plan.

The year after we separated and before the divorce was granted was a huge challenge. My former spouse continued to say unkind things.

Setting up visitation with my sons without engaging in bad conversation with their father was difficult. My former spouse moved out for the last time and my dad's cousin from Florida came up to Illinois to visit my grandmother. My dad's cousin had a heart condition that she kept from her family. While visiting my grandmother, she had a heart attack and was ambulanced to the hospital. For the next few months, she stayed in the hospital, but, unfortunately did not recover. Her oldest son had spoken with my dad and inquired about my situation with my former spouse. My dad told him that it is an awful situation that never improves. My dad shared that I was miserable in the marriage. I will also share that my former spouse was unhappy, too.

My third cousin whom I had not seen since I was nine years old asked about me and how I was doing. I let him know that my marriage was awful, I felt emotionally and spiritually awful, and that nothing improved. He shared how he had been divorced five times. His opinion was to get out of my marriage. I asked if he was recommending divorce because he had been divorced five times. He said, "Not at all. But if it is not working, it is not working." I told him that over the course of 13 years that my family and my church family had listened to me grumble and whine. I could feel they were getting quite tired of it. I said if I decide to end my marriage that I could foresee my former spouse making my life even more difficult. I let my third cousin know that my former spouse was hard for me to emotionally handle. He gave me his phone number and said, "When he causes you grief, you call me." I asked him if he was sure because this is a lot to ask of someone. I said I will likely call you crying and acting like a complete mess. He said that was no problem and to call him, so I did.

When conversations with my sons' dad was not about our sons, I said I had to go and hung up the phone. Other times I just plainly hung up. I learned how to appropriately handle unproductive conversations. I would unplug my landline phone and turn off my cell phone. If there was an unpleasant off-topic text conversation, I would ignore it. Not always did I ignore the text conversation, but when I did, I learned to protect my peace and serenity.

Along my journey, God provided. He provided people and support. My parents helped. My sister and her family helped. My autism support group, my recovery group, my church family and specifically my life group at my church all helped. By definition, a life group consists of four to twenty people gathering in the leader of the group's home or a designated room at the church building, either weekly, bi-weekly, or monthly, to share food, fellowship, Bible study, and prayer. I was blessed one occasion when a woman in my life group came to my house unannounced with several bags of groceries. I was amazed and full of joy. At first I felt undeserving, and she told me that if I did not accept the groceries, I was taking away their blessing of generosity, so I graciously accepted.

Another example of God taking care of our family was receiving an invitation to an autism support group meeting in our community. I was invited at the time my oldest son was nine years old in 2004. I immediately felt the belonging I had wanted for so long as a parent of an autistic boy. The parent meetings were held once a month. I could take both of my sons. Childcare was provided so the parents could freely talk without distraction. Professionals in the field of autism were available for questions. The collective group was amazing. I also grew to find a greater purpose bigger than me to help other parents at the same time they were helping me and my family. Our autism group sponsored autism family movies, zoo and swimming events. We held two fundraisers a year: a golf outing and an autism awareness walk. I joyfully dove into volunteer work within the group and developed lifelong friendships. I felt God's hand when our state announced the launch of a database for urgent needs of services for those with autism.

As a single mom, I had to manage homework and care for my youngest son while tending to the tasking needs of my older autistic son. I was worn-out in the evenings. We successfully got my oldest son and our family on the list. Within a year, my son was granted services. I received respite care services: provided relief for the caregiver of a disabled, sick, or elderly person. After my autistic son's high school graduation, he was able to receive day services under the same program. I have a heart full of gratitude for the autism group and the services my oldest son receives.

My youngest son has had challenges, too. His story is private and not mine to tell. I have seen God's hand in his life. He has overcome so much. My biggest lesson was my inability to believe and have faith that God was going to take care of me and my two sons. God has shown Himself to me over and over. God had nothing to prove. The examples of how God has provided made my faith grow. I worry much less. "Do not be anxious about anything, but in everything by prayer and supplication with thanksgiving, let your requests be made known to God. And the peace of God, which surpasses all understanding, will guard your hearts and your minds in Christ Jesus." Philippians 4:6-7. God has me and my family. The miracles God has provided our family are overflowing.

TERESA D. JOHNSON

Teresa D. Johnson is an insurance professional, blogger, freelance writer, and entrepreneur. Teresa is the lead author in an upcoming book, *Our Life with Autism, the Unexpected Gift: Stories from the Inside.* Teresa was born in central Illinois and lived in Florida and Texas for a short time when she was young. It was during her time in Texas that she discovered her talent for writing and won first place in a statewide academic essay competition at the University of Texas in 1982. She later graduated with a bachelor of arts degree in journalism and political science. She freelanced for the Springfield Business Journal, a monthly business publication from the fall of 2001 to January 2016.

Teresa is an anti-bully advocate supporting Stand for the Silent and a former six-year board member of the Autism Society of America Central Illinois Chapter. She is a single parent to her two sons, Sean and Nick, who reside with her in Taylorville, Illinois. Teresa has a passion to advocate for individuals with autism and their families by providing knowledge to access community services and financial solutions to help bring peace to the entire family.

Connect with Teresa at https://modere.com/7933079.

AFTERWORD

It is our sincere hope that these stories have not only caused you to think, but to ACT! As you read through the transformations, you have seen the authors experience many breakthroughs. We decided to change our lives.

May today be the day you are inspired to choose to create the life you deserve, be courageous enough to act, and surround yourself with inspirational and motivational people who want to see you win.

Today is the perfect day to Take Action!

If any of these stories resonated with you, please connect with the authors. We are here to help you create the life you truly want to live.

With Gratitude,
Dara Bose and Lynda Sunshine West